Picnic of Sounds

OTHER CITATION PRESS BOOKS BY ALBERT CULLUM

Push Back the Desks

Shake Hands with Shakespeare:
Eight Plays for Elementary Schools

Greek Tears and Roman Laughter:
Ten Tragedies and Five Comedies

Aesop in the Afternoon

Picnic of Sounds
A PLAYFUL APPROACH
TO READING

LILLIAN A. BUCKLEY

School of Education

Boston College

ALBERT CULLUM

Dept. of Education

Stonehill College

CITATION PRESS

NEW YORK

1975

LIBRARY OF CONGRESS CATALOGING IN PUBLICATION DATA

Buckley, Lillian A

Picnic of sounds.

1. Language arts (Primary) 2. Educational games.
I. Cullum, Albert, joint author. II. Title.
LB1528.B84 372.6 74-28490
ISBN 0–590–09595–1 (Paper) ISBN 0–590–07430–X (Hdcr.)

Drawings by Lucy Bitzer

PUBLISHED BY CITATION PRESS, LIBRARY AND TRADE DIVISION,
SCHOLASTIC MAGAZINES, INC.
EDITORIAL OFFICE: 50 WEST 44TH STREET, NEW YORK,
NEW YORK 10036.
PRINTED IN THE U.S.A.
LIBRARY OF CONGRESS CATALOG CARD NUMBER: 74-28490

COVER DESIGN BY JACQUELINE CHWAST

1 2 3 4 5 79 78 77 76 75

To classroom teachers who place the magic

before the message

Contents

Section Three: Blends

Section Four: Digraphs

Foreword

Spoken words that transmit ideas, images, needs, wants, and emotions are powerful tools that children enjoy using. Use of oral language must be encouraged and developed in all school programs, from preschool to the highest level of professional education. It is a primary means of acquiring and transmitting knowledge and is often the determining factor in social and professional success.

It is speaking, rather than listening, that really enthralls children; they prefer to be senders rather than receivers of language. With *Picnic of Sounds* children can revel in being language senders. Young children can intelligently echo sentences that carry expressive qualities and satisfying images. They enable them to participate in "reading" short dramatic selections long before they approach the eye languages of reading and writing.

Picnic of Sounds sweeps children so thoroughly into the delights of dramatized situations that one may easily miss the fact that the book emphasizes the relationships between letters and their sounds. Since speech is learned by unconscious imitation—children have no idea of the phonetics of teeth, tongue, lips, and breath control—it is not surprising that the commonest cause of failure in beginning reading is the lack of awareness of separate sounds in speech. Children who have not noticed separate sounds in spoken words or separate words in sentences can make little sense of phonics or reading instruction. It is *awareness* of the elements of sound rather than the ability to repeat words and sentences that is the essential basis for reading. Each playlet in *Picnic of Sounds* is loaded with words that begin with a target letter and stresses the sound through dramatized use of words. Some teachers may find it helpful to print the key words to call attention to the stressed letter. The authors suggest many activities to enrich and utilize the possibilities in the playlets.

The charm and power of *Picnic of Sounds* is its expressive oral language. Children learn by the intake languages of listening and reading, but the output languages of speaking and writing are often neglected in schools. If children are to develop the ability to use speech well, they must have encouragement and practice; it is not acquired in a silent classroom. The authors of *Picnic of Sounds* combine the lilt of dramatization with important prereading skills.

Donald D. Durrell, Professor Emeritus
Boston University

Picnic of Sounds

Why and How This Book

This book is about childhood. It is about running, jumping, yelling, hiding, laughing, crying, scaring and being scared, and being silly. It is a book for teachers and parents, but it's mostly a book for children. It gives children a chance to be all the things they love to be—noisy sometimes, quiet sometimes, scared sometimes, and silly sometimes.

We believe that children are very creative people. Observe them. They create constantly—with blocks, dirt, sand, water, dolls, soapsuds, paint, and with each other. Listen to them. They tell stories. They create situations for dialogue and play the parts of all the characters single-handedly. They take on the roles of others with relish and actually become, for a time, the mommy or the daddy, the army man, the doctor caring for his or her patient, or the teacher directing his or her class. There is virtually no limit to their creativity nor to their love of expressing themselves through dramatic play.

This book provides a number of playlets that can readily be used with children by both teachers and parents. Each playlet is different in spirit. Sometimes children run about, sometimes they shout for joy (louder and louder), sometimes they are scared, and sometimes they are very, very quiet. Every emotion of life is touched upon at one time or another.

If you are a parent using this book, you might just read the playlets with your child and enjoy the sense of sharing and closeness that exists when child and parent read together. The playlets are uncomplicated in both language and concept and—very obvious—instantly understood and very soon learned and chanted from memory.

If you are a teacher using this book, you will find many uses for the playlets depending upon the sophistication of the children in your classroom. The playlets, by their very nature, get children quickly involved—talking, moving, feeling.

When children first come to school, they come full of the expectation that life in school is going to be as good or even better than life before school. However, they also come somewhat frightened and apprehensive. What better way to allay these fears and apprehensions and get everyone communicating with everyone else than by passing around a big pot while chanting,

> Lamb chops, pork chops, and chocolate chips.
> Step right up and wet your lips.
> Chew! Chomp! Chew and chomp!
> Chew! Chomp! Chew and chomp!

Then everyone gets to "chew and chomp" his or her own chocolate chip cookie! *Everyone* eats, *everyone* chants, *everyone* has fun, and *everyone* has something exciting to tell about when an adult asks, "What did you do in school today?"

One of the major concerns of teachers of young children is the initiation of reading instruction. Prior to the time children begin formal instruction, considerable attention is paid to teaching and learning certain readiness skills. It is generally known, as a result of extensive research, that to be successful in learning to read, children must be proficient in a number of different skills and abilities. High on the list of these skills and abilities necessary for success in beginning reading is the capacity to differentiate the separate sounds in spoken words. Depending on the capabilities of individual children, differing amounts of practice are necessary to insure mastery in this area. Providing varying, short practices is imperative so that children do not become bored and disinterested. We feel that this book can be a great help in this area. It provides practice—practice in hearing the separate sounds in spoken words. Each playlet concentrates on a particular sound. Through listening to and acting out any one playlet, children hear and say a great number of words containing a specific sound. For example, the playlet entitled *Maybe* contains six different words beginning with the *m* sound, and, through repetition, sixteen words beginning with *m* are heard and said by the children.

Repetition is the key word here. Children in their earliest years learn through mimicry and repetition. They mimic the expressions and actions of the nurturing adults in their lives. They repeat over and over the favorite verses of Mother Goose. And what child does not delight in repeating the phrases "once upon a time" and "they lived happily ever after" as often as possible? They learn these expressions, poems, and phrases incidentally and informally, merely through the repetition of them. So, too, will they learn the lines of the playlets in this book, incidentally and informally, through repetition.

It is suggested that teachers using these playlets with young children in the classroom first be very familiar with each playlet and knowledgeable of the possibilities for enacting each within the confines of their own classrooms. We believe it is best to first read each playlet to the children in its entirety. Since there is an occasional "big word" (used intentionally to expand vocabulary), these should be brought to the attention of the children to ensure understanding of all the words.

Comments should be encouraged and engaged in freely. If the playlet is silly, why is it silly? If it is scary, what makes it scary? Similar situations experienced by the children (if there are any) can be talked about and duly noted. It is through the short discussions about a playlet that children feel their first personal involvement in the story line and the characterizations. Everyone should be helped to participate so that everyone will have a part in the "performance."

A second reading of the playlet is recommended following the discussion. During the second reading, the goal of the teacher should be to create an atmosphere that will enhance the enjoyment of the children and prepare them for their own performances.

Atmosphere can be created easily through the use of gestures, facial expressions, and appropriate use of the voice. For example, when a playlet is funny or ridiculous, the voice should be warm, light and "chuckly." When the situation is scary or suspenseful, the teacher might "intone" the lines and "act" very scared by shuddering or quaking.

Children are natural actors and actresses. They will immediately respond to the atmosphere created. The atmosphere, then, must be replete with emotion, with a sense of the larger than life, with a sense of theater!

Once the children are familiar with a playlet, the teacher will have no difficulty getting volunteers to assume certain roles or be members of the chorus. Parts can be gone over, line by line, very quickly before movement is added. One of the greatest strengths of the playlets is that their content will not overwhelm the actors and actresses. No one person has a great deal to say, but *all* have *something* to say.

On the first enactment of each playlet, it is recommended that the children "walk through" the actions saying their lines. Once this is done, they are ready to give full vent to the emotions inherent in each playlet. Always emphasize movement and emotion. Be prepared to let children shout or laugh or run or jump in the air or be scared or whisper. Once they have enacted the playlet a time or two, are comfortable with its structure, and feel self-assured, they will act out the playlet over and over again on their own—until a new playlet is introduced. And, if they are like the children with whom we have used these playlets, they will come up with many more suggestions for staging and acting all by themselves!

When children are further along in the process of beginning reading, they can review each playlet as it becomes appropriate and determine which words contain the specific sound being reviewed. Saying each word orally and hearing each said provides children a way of becoming both more aware of the sound itself and to recognize the sound when it is heard in different words.

As children become more advanced, they will be able to write the words containing a particular sound from any playlet and check their own spelling of the words by consulting the book themselves. Each playlet is followed by a listing of all the words used in it that contain the sound being practiced. And how much more meaningful spelling becomes because of all the emotions and experiences already attached to these words!

Older children can use this book independently and stage their own productions for audiences using the suggestions for staging that accompany each playlet. Children retain a sense of fun and a sense of the absurd throughout childhood and, therefore, these playlets are very appropriate for dramatic presentations even in the upper grades.

Lastly, we have included a section entitled Enrichment Activities to accompany each playlet. These were designed to extend the enjoyment for children and to provide both parents and teachers with ideas to further involve children in meaningful, for-fun activities.

So, come, participate once again in childhood. Determine the needs of the children you know and use this book to their best advantage. Join them and do some running or laughing or scaring or hiding yourself. Your life and the lives of your children can only be richer for it.

Section One:
CONSONANTS

b	c	d	f
g	h	j	k
l	m	n	p
r	s	t	v
w	y	z	

꙳ SUGGESTIONS FOR STAGING

Solos 1 and 2 stand in front of the class. They can actually display their belly buttons or point through their clothes. On line 3 everyone stands to point to his or her belly button.

꙳ SUGGESTIONS FOR INTERPRETATION

After line 7 solos 1 and 2 parade and strut about the room pointing to their belly buttons.

꙳ SUGGESTIONS FOR ENRICHMENT

Draw babies in diapers with belly buttons.

Draw all types of balls—Christmas balls, baseballs, basketballs, footballs, and the like.

Discuss things that bounce and things that bend.

Create a bulletin board with pictures of each child as a baby.

Bring in pictures of people whose belly buttons are in view.

Have a button exhibit. The children can bring in unusual buttons from home to display.

Belly button

b

1. **Belly button, belly button** (solos 1 and 2)
2. On my tummy wall. (solos 1 and 2)
3. **Belly button, belly button** (all)
4. Like a little **ball.** (all)
5. It can't **bounce.** (half the class)
6. It won't **bend.** (other half)
7. And it follows me like a friend. (solos 1 and 2)

✑§ REVIEW OF WORDS

belly	ball	bend
button	bounce	

✑ SUGGESTIONS FOR STAGING

The teacher should actually glue or tape a penny to the ceiling. Solo 1 looks up at the penny, and on line 4 the class also looks up and points to the penny stuck to the ceiling.

✑ SUGGESTIONS FOR INTERPRETATION

Solo 1 is upset about the cent stuck to ceiling. Solo 2, a centipede, comes in from the hallway crawling slowly, stops, delivers line 6, and slowly crawls back to the hallway. Solo 1 begins to cry on line 8 and builds up to very distressing crying on lines 9 and 10.

✑ SUGGESTIONS FOR ENRICHMENT

While the class hide their faces on their tables or desks, children can take turns deciding where the penny should be glued on the ceiling. See how long it takes everyone in the class to locate the penny on the ceiling.

Invite others to come in and see if they notice anything on the ceiling.

Give each child a penny and ask what they observe about it.

The cent on the ceiling

C

1. I threw a **cent** up in the air. (solo 1)
2. It's stuck to the **ceiling**! (all)
3. I threw a **cent** up in the air. (solo 1)
4. And there it is . . . stuck to the **ceiling**! (all)
5. A **centipede** came walking by. (all)
6. Oh, my gosh! There's a **cent** on the **ceiling**! (solo 2)
7. And then he walked away. (all)
8. My **cent**! (solo 1)
9. My last **cent**! (solo 1)
10. My only **cent**! (solo 1)
11. Stuck to the **ceiling**!!! (all)

∽ß REVIEW OF WORDS

cent	ceiling	centipede

◄§ SUGGESTIONS FOR STAGING

Solos 1, 2, 3, and 4 hide behind something and step out to make their announcements at the right time. On line 3 the class rushes to the front of the room to accept the food and then return to their seats. The same process is repeated on lines 6 and 9.

◄§ SUGGESTIONS FOR INTERPRETATION

Solos 1, 2, 3, and 4 make their announcements loudly and clearly as if they are barkers at a circus. The class is very excited on lines 3, 6, and 9 and very disgusted on line 12.

◄§ SUGGESTIONS FOR ENRICHMENT

Draw pictures of cotton candy, a frosted cake, corn on the cob, and carrots.

Discuss birthdays and birthday cakes.

Discuss picnics and eating corn on the cob.

Discuss carrots being nutritious and good for one.

Bring in a popper and pop corn in the classroom. Add butter and salt and enjoy, enjoy!

Bring in a cupcake for each child and make instant frosting in the classroom. Each child can scoop some frosting onto his cupcake, spread it around, and eat it.

*Come
and
get it*

C

1. **Cotton candy! Cotton candy!** (solo 1)
2. **Come** and get it! **Come** and get it! (solo 1)
3. Oh, that yummy **cotton candy!** (all)
4. The **cake** is frosted! The **cake** is frosted! (solo 2)
5. **Come** and get it! **Come** and get it! (solo 2)
6. Oh, that sweet frosted **cake!** (all)
7. The **corn** is **cooked!** The **corn** is **cooked!** (solo 3)
8. **Come** and get it! **Come** and get it! (solo 3)
9. Oh, we love that **corn** on the **cob!** (all)
10. The **carrots** are ready! The **carrots** are ready! (solo 4)
11. **Come** and get them! **Come** and get them! (solo 4)
12. UGH! (all)

✑ REVIEW OF WORDS

cotton	cake	cob
candy	corn	carrots
come	cooked	

SUGGESTIONS FOR STAGING

Solos 1, 2, 3, and 4 should hide and appear only to scold the class.

SUGGESTIONS FOR INTERPRETATION

The solo characters could dress up as grownups simply by wearing a hat or an apron. The class becomes increasingly annoyed with each command from the authority figures. The whole class should stand and exclaim loudly on line 9.

SUGGESTIONS FOR ENRICHMENT

Draw authority figures with long extended fingers pointing and scolding.

Discuss do rules and don't rules for children, and then discuss do rules and don't rules they think should apply to parents and teachers as well.

Make a list of things children would like to be able to do. Follow this up with a list of things they don't want parents to do.

Let the children draw pictures of themselves doing something they know their parents disapprove of. The teacher can write what a parent would say on the bottom of the picture.

Make a list of all the things the boys and girls are going to let their children do when they become parents.

Don't do this
and don't
do that

1. **Don't dunk** the **doughnuts!** (solo 1)
2. **Don't do** this and **don't do** that! (all)
3. **Don't dump** the **dominoes!** (solo 2)
4. **Don't do** this and **don't do** that! (all)
5. **Don't dig** the **dirt!** (solo 3)
6. **Don't do** this and **don't do** that! (all)
7. **Don't** bother **daddy!** (solo 4)
8. **Don't do** this and **don't do** that! (all)
9. All they say is **don't!** (all)

⋙ REVIEW OF WORDS

don't	doughnuts	dig
do	dump	dirt
dunk	dominoes	daddy

ᴥᏭ   SUGGESTIONS FOR STAGING

Four fish are in a corner and they begin to swim about the room. A baby fish waits to be born in another corner. On line 12 half the class slowly rise, slowly move toward the fish, and slowly wave their arms. On line 13 the other half does the same. On line 14 the waving arms of the fog cover the fish.

ᴥᏭ   SUGGESTIONS FOR INTERPRETATION

The four fish should be encouraged to be very silly and fidgety. Lines 3, 4, 5, 8, 9, and 10 should sound ludicrous! Lines 11, 12, 13, and 14 should be very slow and threatening. Line 16 is extremely slow and drawn out. Turning out the lights would help create atmosphere.

ᴥᏭ   SUGGESTIONS FOR ENRICHMENT

Draw funny faces.

Have a goldfish day in the classroom.

Read the poem "Fog" by Carl Sandburg.

Make word lists of feelings one has on dark, foggy nights.

Get materials and put together a class aquarium. Look in books to determine which fish are best for the aquarium.

Write class or individual haikus about fog.

Four funny fish

1. **Four funny, funny, fidgety fish** (all)
2. Went looking **for fun!** (all)
3. **Fun** and **fudge!** (solos 1, 2, 3, and 4)
4. **Fun** and **fudge!** (solos 1, 2, 3, and 4)
5. **Fun** and **fudge!** (solos 1, 2, 3, and 4)
6. **Four funny, funny, fidgety fish** (all)
7. Went looking **for fun!** (all)
8. **Fun** and **fudge!** (solos 1, 2, 3, and 4)
9. **Fun** and **fudge!** (solos 1, 2, 3, and 4)
10. **Fun** and **fudge!** (solos 1, 2, 3, and 4)
11. But they got lost in the **fog!** (all)
12. Misty **fog**. (half the class)
13. Heavy **fog!** (other half)
14. Slow moving **fog**. (all)
15. Look! One **fish** had a baby **fish!** (solo 5)
16. **Five funny, fidgety fish** are lost in the **fog!** (all)

REVIEW OF WORDS

four	fish	fudge
funny	for	fog
fidgety	fun	five

SUGGESTIONS FOR STAGING

Solos 1 and 2 stand in front of the room. George could be holding a plate or cup or something breakable that is not valuable.

SUGGESTIONS FOR INTERPRETATION

On line 7 solos 2 and 3 pull the object back and forth. On line 9 solos 2 and 4 pull the object back and forth. It falls to the floor after line 10. Line 11 should be extremely loud! On line 12 the three solos are very disgusted with George.

SUGGESTIONS FOR ENRICHMENT

Draw gentle animals.

Make an outline of a large giraffe. A spot can be added by each child as she or he says a word that begins with a soft g.

Play an imaginary game: "I gently hand this gentle animal to you. What is it?" The child receiving the animal can ask questions such as: "Is it soft?" or "Does it have a long tail?"

Oh, George!

g

1. **George,** carry it **gently.** (solo 1)
2. Carry it **gently George.** (all)
3. I am carrying it **gently!** (solo 2)
4. **George,** carry it **gently.** (solo 1)
5. Carry it **gently George.** (all)
6. I am carrying it **gently.** (solo 2)
7. Let me hold it **George.** (solo 3)
8. No! No! No! (solo 2)
9. Let me hold it **George.** (solo 4)
10. No! No! No! (solo 2)
11. CRASH!!! (all)
12. Oh, **George!** (solos 1, 3, and 4)

≈§ REVIEW OF WORDS

George   gently

ৡ৳   SUGGESTIONS FOR STAGING

Solo 4 waits in the front of the room to speak the final punch line. Solos 1, 2, and 3 stand to speak their lines.

ৡ৳   SUGGESTIONS FOR INTERPRETATION

The garage could be under a table at the front of the room. The teacher or a student can represent the goat and let the young goose sit on his or her back during lines 6 to 10. Encourage the goose to blow a bubble on line 15. After line 16 the goose could quack all around the room acting as goofy and goony as the child likes.

ৡ৳   SUGGESTIONS FOR ENRICHMENT

At the end of the day the children can leave the room and go home as waddling geese.

Draw geese doing silly things.

Discuss how geese migrate from cold weather to warm weather and how they fly in the sky in a "v" formation. Children can fly about the schoolyard in such a manner.

That goofy goose

1. Look at that **goose**! (all)
2. Look at that **goose**! (all)
3. Look at that **goofy goose**! (all)
4. Oh, wow! What's the **goose** doing now? (solo 1)
5. The **goofy goose** is in the **garage**! (all)
6. Look at that **goose**! (all)
7. Look at that **goose**! (all)
8. Look at that **goofy goose**! (all)
9. Oh, wow! What's the **goose** doing now? (solo 2)
10. The **goofy goose** is sitting on the **goat**! (all)
11. Look at that **goose**! (all)
12. Look at that **goose**! (all)
13. Look at that **goofy goose**! (all)
14. Oh, wow! What's the **goose** doing now? (solo 3)
15. The **goofy goose** is blowing bubbles with my bubble **gum**! (all)
16. I **guess** I'm a **goofy**, **goony goose**!!! (solo 4)

⮑ REVIEW OF WORDS

goose	goat	guess
goofy	gum	goony
garage		

◄§ SUGGESTIONS FOR STAGING

Children playing the three solo parts should be huddled in a corner very quiet and sad. The rest of the class sit at their desks or tables. On line 1 the class stands. At line 2 the class takes a hop toward the huddled three and continues to hop closer and closer on each successive line. At line 9 the huddled three jump up.

◄§ SUGGESTIONS FOR INTERPRETATION

The class should be very gentle and make every attempt to cheer up the huddled three, who are very emotional and upset. On line 16 they cry and wail.

◄§ SUGGESTIONS FOR ENRICHMENT

Draw hurt heads, hands, and other parts of the body. The classroom could become a temporary hospital as doctors and nurses diagnose each hurt case.

Play hopscotch in the playground or in the room by marking the floor with tape.

List things that hurt people on the outside (falling down) and things that hurt on the inside (a friend not talking to us).

Read stories about the jobs performed by doctors and nurses.

Discuss why some children fear doctors and don't want to go for their checkups.

Small Band-Aids can be given to the children to wear for the day.

Boo hoo!
boo hoo!

h

1. Don't be sad. (all)
2. **Hop** and be **happy.** (all)
3. **Hop** and be **happy.** (all)
4. **Hopscotch? Hopscotch?** (all)
5. Don't be sad. (all)
6. **Hippity hop.** (all)
7. **Hippity hop.** (all)
8. **Hopscotch? Hopscotch?** (all)
9. Stop! (solos 1, 2, and 3)
10. We are sad! (solos 1, 2, and 3)
11. We **hurt** ourselves! (solos 1, 2, and 3)
12. **Hurt! Hurt! Hurt!** (solos 1, 2, and 3)
13. My finger **hurts!** (solo 1)
14. My **head hurts!** (solo 2)
15. My **hand hurts!** (solo 3)
16. Boo **hoo!** Boo **hoo!** Boo **hoo!** (solos 1, 2, and 3)

◄§ REVIEW OF WORDS

hop	hippity	hand
happy	hurt	hoo
hopscotch	head	

◄§ SUGGESTIONS FOR STAGING

Three students are chosen to represent Jimmy, Judy, and Johnny. The wastepaper basket could represent the jelly jar. Each solo part waits for the command to jump.

◄§ SUGGESTIONS FOR INTERPRETATION

Each jumper can use any style of jumping—the more dramatic, the better. When Johnny misses and lands in the middle of the jelly jar, he can cry or scream or yell or moan. On line 9 solo 3 jumps up to deliver his line. On line 10 the whole class gathers around the jelly jar to look at Johnny covered with jelly.

◄§ SUGGESTIONS FOR ENRICHMENT

Draw jars filled with delicious candies.

The teacher could give each student a small taste of grape or apple jelly.

Read another jumping poem such as "Jack Be Nimble."

Draw pictures, look in books, and make lists of animals that jump to get around.

List fruits that can be made into jelly. The teacher might bring in an unusual jelly such as persimmon.

Discuss what Johnny felt like when he failed to jump over the jar. What is the important thing for Johnny (or anyone) to do? Try again.

Make a list of items stored in jars in mothers' cabinets.

Write a letter to a manufacturer to find out why some things are packaged in cans and other things are in glass or plastic jars.

Jiggly jelly

1. **Jump** over the **jelly jar**. (solo 1)
2. **Jump** over the **jelly jar**. (all)
3. Don't be a **jerk**! (solo 2)
4. Don't be a **jerk**! (all)
5. **Jump** over the **jelly jar**! (all)
6. Watch **Jimmy jump**! (all)
7. Watch **Judy jump**! (all)
8. Watch **Johnny jump**! (all)
9. **Johnny** missed! (solo 3)
10. **Johnny's** covered with **jiggly jelly**! (all)

✒ REVIEW OF WORDS

jump	jerk	Johnny
jelly	Jimmy	jiggly
jar	Judy	

～§ SUGGESTIONS FOR STAGING

The kitten can be imaginary or a pupil can play the role. Items could be on a table, using blocks instead of a kettle and a bottle of ketchup. Solo 1 could be out of sight if it's an imaginary kitchen with an imaginary kitten.

～§ SUGGESTIONS FOR INTERPRETATION

Tension and excitement should build as the kitten gets closer and closer to trouble. Very loud on line 7! Line 9 as loud as possible by solo 1. Much laughter on line 10!

～§ SUGGESTIONS FOR ENRICHMENT

Make humorous drawings of a kitchen covered with ketchup.

Hunt for kitten pictures at home.

Draw a huge ketchup bottle.

Describe a kitten as mischievous, and list other activities of both animals and children that would be considered mischievous.

Have a series of kitten days during which children can bring their kittens or cats to school and tell about them.

*The kitten
in the kitchen*

k

1. The **kitten** is near the **kitchen**. (half the class)
2. Oh, oh! Oh, oh! Oh, oh! (half the class)
3. The **kitten** is in the **kitchen**. (other half)
4. Oh, oh! Oh, oh! Oh, oh! (other half)
5. The **kitten** is near the **kettle**. (half the class)
6. Oh, oh! Oh, oh! Oh, oh! (half the class)
7. The **kitten** is near the **ketchup**. (other half)
8. Oh, oh! Oh, oh! Oh, oh! (other half)
9. Crash! (solo 1)
10. The **kitten** is covered with **ketchup**! (all)

✑§ REVIEW OF WORDS

kitten	kettle	ketchup
kitchen		

✎§ SUGGESTIONS FOR STAGING

Everyone is in his or her seat holding an imaginary gigantic lollipop.

✎§ SUGGESTIONS FOR INTERPRETATION

Before they begin, each child can state what color or flavor his lollipop is. The licking should be done loudly and in unison. Line 1 should be very loud, and the volume then diminishes to soft on line 9. Line 11 is very sad and line 12 very sad and tearful.

✎§ SUGGESTIONS FOR ENRICHMENT

Draw huge colorful lollipops.

Throw a real lollipop party.

Develop the concept of comparisons: little, littler, littlest and big, bigger, biggest.

Make a lollipop monster (fashioned after a Sesame Street monster) with a big open mouth and a bag attached to the back. Words can be written on paper lollipops, and the children must say the words to feed the lollipop monster.

Make lollipops in school. Needed: hot plate, double boiler, medium-sized bowl, wooden skewers, and wooden spoon. One recipe for about 20 lollipops is:

Melt 50 caramels and 6 tbs water in top of double boiler, stirring occasionally until caramels are melted. Put 8 cups of Rice Krispies in the bowl and pour caramel mixture over them; stir with wooden spoon until cereal is well coated.

With greased hands pack cereal mixture into round balls; insert wooden skewer into center of each. Place on waxed paper and leave in school refrigerator or outside window in cold weather for half an hour.

Lollipop time

1. We have big, big, big **lollipops**. (all)
2. **Lick, lick, lick**. (all)
3. We have big **lollipops**. (all)
4. **Lick, lick, lick**. (all)
5. We have **lollipops**. (all)
6. **Lick, lick, lick**. (all)
7. We have **little lollipops**. (all)
8. **Lick, lick, lick**. (all)
9. We have **little, little, little lollipops**. (all)
10. **Lick, lick, lick**. (all)
11. Oh! (all)
12. We **licked** our **lollipops** away! (all)

◆§ REVIEW OF WORDS

lollipops	little	licked
lick		

~§ SUGGESTIONS FOR STAGING

Speak lines 1 and 2 from the front of the room and lines 3 and 4 from the back of the room. Solo 2 delivers lines 6 and 7 from one side of the room and lines 8 and 9 from the other side of the room. Lines 11 and 12 can be said from behind the teacher's desk and lines 13 and 14 from in front of the desk. The class's responses are: lines 5 and 10 sitting and line 15 standing!

~§ SUGGESTIONS FOR INTERPRETATION

The solo parts will enjoy "acting up a storm" as authority figures. They should show much annoyance. The class's responses should increase in volume with line 15 extremely rebellious and angry.

~§ SUGGESTIONS FOR ENRICHMENT

Students can draw pictures of authority figures making demands and commands, such as mother commands, father commands, grandparent commands, and teacher commands. The teacher can write in the commands of the playlet.

Have each child ask his parents what "bugs" them most. Compile a list or make a series of labeled drawings describing parents' dislikes.

Discuss why parents get upset over some things their children do, such as making messy rooms or a great deal of noise.

Plan some role-playing situations in which children can practice manners or courtesies, such as telephoning and making introductions.

Tape children imitating parents telling them to clean up their rooms or hang up their clothes.

Maybe

m

1. Your room is **messy**! (solo 1)
2. Your room is **messy**! (solo 1)
3. Clean it up! (solo 1)
4. Clean it up! (solo 1)
5. **Maybe** we will! **Maybe** we won't! (all)
6. You **must** eat your **meat**! (solo 2)
7. You **must** eat your **meat**! (solo 2)
8. Eat it up! (solo 2)
9. Eat it up! (solo 2)
10. **Maybe** we will! **Maybe** we won't! (all)
11. **Mind** your **manners**! (solo 3)
12. **Mind** your **manners**! (solo 3)
13. Do you hear **me**? (solo 3)
14. Do you hear **me**? (solo 3)
15. **Maybe** we do! **Maybe** we don't! (all)

REVIEW OF WORDS

messy	meat	manners
maybe	mind	me
must		

SUGGESTIONS FOR STAGING

On lines 1 and 2 solo 1 runs to the front of the room. On lines 4 and 5 solo 2 runs to the front of the room. On line 8 the class begins to get excited. On lines 9 and 10 everyone stands up. On line 11 everyone runs to a corner of the room except solo 3, who on line 12 opens the classroom door, looks out into the hallway, and announces his discovery. Line 13 is very, very loud from everyone!

SUGGESTIONS FOR INTERPRETATION

The solo parts should attempt to create an atmosphere of fear. When in the corners of the room the students should be trembling with fear . . . very exaggerated!

SUGGESTIONS FOR ENRICHMENT

Encourage the children to bring in all kinds of false noses. The teacher should also wear a fake nose on this occasion.

Children can draw all kinds of noses—human noses, animal noses, monster noses!

Discuss what each child would do if he or she were home alone and heard a noise outside that kept getting louder and louder.

Let the children draw pictures of themselves with very bad colds. Words describing how they feel can be added along the bottom of the picture.

Tape record various kerchoos. Play them back and see if the kerchooers can be identified.

Kerchoo!

n

1. Listen! (solo 1)
2. I hear a **noise**! (solo 1)
3. We didn't hear a **noise**. (all)
4. Listen! (solo 2)
5. The **noise** is getting **nearer**! (solo 2)
6. We still don't hear a **noise**. (all)
7. Listen! Listen! Listen! (solos 1 and 2)
8. The **noise** is getting **nearer**! (all)
9. The **noise** is **near**! (all)
10. The **noise** is here! (all)
11. The **noise** is **now**! (all)
12. Oh, it's just a big **nose** that sneezed. (solo 3)
13. Kerchoo! (all)

REVIEW OF WORDS

listen	nearer	now
noise	near	nose

✥ SUGGESTIONS FOR STAGING

Divide the class into five sections and make one big circle. As each group presents its line, it steps into the center of the circle.

✥ SUGGESTIONS FOR INTERPRETATION

Group 1 should begin very softly, and as each group enters the center of the circle, it will naturally speak louder and louder. Line 9 again will be very, very soft. The teacher can be the orchestra leader to indicate when to increase or diminish the tempo and volume of the raindrops.

✥ SUGGESTIONS FOR ENRICHMENT

Listen to rain records such as "Raindrops Keep Falling on My Head."

Draw a rainstorm.

Discuss the sadness of rainy days and having to stay inside.

Read rain poems.

Put a bucket outside on a rainy day and measure how much water accumulates by the end of the day.

Make a list of things that like the rain (ducks, flowers) and a list of things that don't like the rain (picnic-goers, me!)

Put on raincoats and hats on a rainy day and go outside to look around the school or to say a rainy day poem.

A rainy day

p

1. **Pit, pit, pit, pit.** (group 1)
2. **Pat, pat, pat, pat.** (groups 1 and 2)
3. **Pitter, pitter, pitter, pitter.** (groups 1, 2, and 3)
4. **Patter, patter, patter, patter.** (groups 1, 2, 3, and 4)
5. **Pitter, patter, pitter, patter.** (groups 1, 2, 3, 4, and 5)
6. **Patter, patter, patter, patter.** (groups 1, 2, 3, and 4)
7. **Pitter, pitter, pitter, pitter.** (groups 1, 2, and 3)
8. **Pat, pat, pat, pat.** (groups 1 and 2)
9. **Pit, pit, pit, pit.** (group 1)

ها REVIEW OF WORDS

pit	pitter	patter
pat		

∾ SUGGESTIONS FOR STAGING

Children should all be seated on the floor. After line 3 solo 1 flips over and begins to swim around on the floor. All others follow suit. After line 6 children jump around and after line 9 they skip. After line 12 children fall in a heap on the floor and pretend to sleep. The teacher can blow a whistle to indicate when to stop each activity.

∾ SUGGESTIONS FOR INTERPRETATION

Children should be encouraged to do each activity vigorously. Solos must remember to give sharp, loud commands for the "Do this" lines.

∾ SUGGESTIONS FOR ENRICHMENT

Have a jumping contest on a grassy area outside the school. Let children practice and then see who can jump the farthest.

Have children "dream" while they pretend to sleep. Talk about what they dreamed then and at other times. Discuss nightmares.

Make up other rickety racketies to teach rhyming words.

Rickety rackety

1. **Rickety, rackety, rim!** (all)
2. Boy! I love to swim. (solo 1)
3. Do this! (solo 1)
4. **Rickety, rackety, rump!** (all)
5. Boy! I love to jump. (solo 2)
6. Do this! (solo 2)
7. **Rickety, rackety, rip!** (all)
8. Boy! I love to skip. (solo 3)
9. Do this! (solo 3)
10. **Rickety, rackety, reep!** (all)
11. We're **tired!** Let us sleep! (all)
12. Do this! (solo 4)

◆§ REVIEW OF WORDS

rickety	rump	reep
rackety	rip	tired
rim		

SUGGESTIONS FOR STAGING

The class should line up against the wall waiting for the bus to arrive. Solos 1 and 3 pretend they are driving a bus that starts from another part of the room. The honks sound far away at first, then louder, and then fade away as the bus vanishes into the distance.

SUGGESTIONS FOR INTERPRETATION

Much enthusiastic excitement for lines 3, 4, and 5 and much sadness on lines 8 and 9. Similarly much excitement for lines 12, 13, and 14 and sadness on lines 17, 18, and 19. On line 19 the class should sit on the floor in a state of dejection.

SUGGESTIONS FOR ENRICHMENT

Draw all types of buses.

A bus driver could visit the class for a few minutes and answer questions the children have about buses and driving.

The teacher might obtain a bus driver's cap for children to take turns wearing.

Talk about how children would feel if they were running to catch the school bus in the morning and missed it. Build a list of words describing their feelings.

Make a neighborhood map and place on it pictures of the children's houses or apartments and other landmarks. Homes may be labeled so children will know where others live.

Draw a big bus on mural paper. Cut out windows and let the children draw themselves or cut out pictures and stick them in the windows of the bus.

Write a fantasy story about where a magic bus might go and what its riders might do on a magic trip.

Honk! honk! **S**

1. Honk! Honk! (solo 1)
2. Honk! Honk! (solo 1)
3. Here **comes** the **bus**. (all)
4. The **bus** is big. (all)
5. The **bus** is **busy**! (all)
6. Honk! Honk! (solo 1)
7. Honk! Honk! (solo 1)
8. Oh! We **missed** the **bus**! (solo 2)
9. We **missed** that **busy bus**. (all)
10. Honk! Honk! (solo 3)
11. Honk! Honk! (solo 3)
12. Here **comes** another **bus**. (all)
13. **This bus** is big. (all)
14. **This bus** is **busy**. (all)
15. Honk! Honk! (solo 3)
16. Honk! Honk! (solo 3)
17. Oh! We **missed** the **second bus**. (solo 2)
18. We **missed** the **second busy bus**! (all)
19. And it **was** the **last** big, **busy bus** of the day! (all)

⋙ REVIEW OF WORDS

comes	busy	second
bus	missed	was
is	this	last

◆§ SUGGESTIONS FOR STAGING

Establish an imaginary room in front of the class. A table and some chairs will help. Solos 1, 2, and 3 can be in various corners of the room ready to find their hiding place. Solo 4 enters from the corridor on line 7.

◆§ SUGGESTIONS FOR INTERPRETATION

The class says its lines in a very quiet mysterious manner. Solo 1 imitates a tiger, solo 2 imitates a turtle, and solo 3 imitates a toad. Darkening the room as much as possible would be fun! On line 9 the three animals jump out and frighten solo 4 with a very loud BOO!

◆§ SUGGESTIONS FOR ENRICHMENT

Collect pictures of animals that begin with the *t* sound. Draw *t* sound animals hiding.

Make tiger tails, construct paper turtle backs complete with markings, and make head masks with bulging eyes for the toads.

Play other tiptoe games, for example, get the doggie's bone.

Have someone bring in toe shoes from dancing class. Let the children try them on and then try walking and dancing on toe points.

Tiptoe, tiptoe

1. **Tiptoe, tiptoe** quietly as a **tiger**. (all)
2. **Tiptoe, tiptoe** down the stairs. (solo 1)
3. **Tiptoe, tiptoe** quietly as a **turtle**. (all)
4. **Tiptoe, tiptoe** underneath the **table**. (solo 2)
5. **Tiptoe, tiptoe** quietly as a **toad**. (all)
6. **Tiptoe, tiptoe** behind the **television**. (solo 3)
7. **Tiptoe, tiptoe** quietly as me. (solo 4)
8. **Tiptoe, tiptoe** into the room. (solo 4)
9. BOO! (solos 1, 2, and 3)

❧ REVIEW OF WORDS

tiptoe	turtle	television
tiger	table	into
	toad	

⋖§ SUGGESTIONS FOR STAGING

The vase, violin, and vacuum can be imaginary or real items located in various parts of the room. As Virginia and Vincent go to each respective place, the class responds.

⋖§ SUGGESTIONS FOR INTERPRETATION

The class becomes progressively annoyed with Vincent and Virginia, and by line 8 they are extremely angry and pronounce the sentence in line 9 with dramatic gusto.

⋖§ SUGGESTIONS FOR ENRICHMENT

Draw Vincent and Virginia crying big tears.

Bring a real vacuum cleaner into the classroom. As the children give the teacher words beginning with the letter *v*, she writes each on a small piece of paper that she places on the floor. Different children can take turns holding the vacuum cleaner hose and scooping the *v* words into the vacuum cleaner.

Children can flip through magazines looking for pictures of faces depicting different emotions such as anger, happiness, sadness, and the like. They can cut out the faces and mount them on a bulletin board or in a scrapbook.

They
did not
obey

V

1. **Vincent**! **Virginia**! (all)
2. Don't touch the **vase**! (all)
3. **Vincent**! **Virginia**! (all)
4. Don't play with the **violin**! (all)
5. **Vincent**! **Virginia**! (all)
6. Don't turn on the **vacuum**! (all)
7. But . . . **Vincent** and **Virginia** did not obey! (solos 1 and 2)
8. Soooooooooo! (all)
9. No **TV** for one whole year! (all)

✌§ REVIEW OF WORDS

Vincent	vase	vacuum
Virginia	violin	TV

SUGGESTIONS FOR STAGING

The children sit at their seats moving their arms and presenting their lines in a windy fashion. Solo 1 speaks from underneath a desk. Solo 2 flies away after stating his line. Solo 3 stands erect with his or her arms outstretched. Solo 4 waits outside the classroom for his cue to enter.

SUGGESTIONS FOR INTERPRETATION

The class speaks the wind's lines very pleadingly. Line 10 is very, very sad. The class stands on line 14 and, joined by solo 4, the children begin to wander all over the room in an orderly fashion. It would be fun if they could wander into the hallway, the principal's office, and then outside.

SUGGESTIONS FOR ENRICHMENT

Draw big wind storms with things flying through the air such as chairs, bathtubs, cars, and barns.

Read to the class wind poems such as Christina Rossetti's "Who Has Seen the Wind?"

Discuss with the class the funny tricks the wind can play on people!

Tell the Aesop fable of the man and the satyr in which the satyr is confused by the man blowing on his hands to warm them up and then on his soup to cool it.

Read the first chapter of *The Wizard of Oz* and talk about the tornado that blew Dorothy from Kansas to the land of Oz.

The wandering wind

W

1. **Wander with** me. **Wander with** me. (all)
2. **Wander with** me **wooden wagon.** (all)
3. No, **Winter Wind!** No! (solo 1)
4. **Wander with** me. **Wander with** me. (all)
5. **Wander with** me Mr. **Woodpecker.** (all)
6. No, **Winter Wind!** No! (solo 2)
7. **Wander with** me. **Wander with** me. (all)
8. **Wander with** me **woolen** cape. (all)
9. No, **Winter Wind!** No! (solo 3)
10. I guess I'll **wander** alone. (all)
11. **Wait, Winter Wind! Wait. Wait.** (solo 4)
12. I'll **wander with** you. (solo 4)
13. Hurry, **William** . . . hurry. (all)
14. And they **wandered** all over the **world.** (all)

🕭 REVIEW OF WORDS

wander	winter	wait
with	wind	William
wooden	woodpecker	wandered
wagon	woolen	world

❧ SUGGESTIONS FOR STAGING

One third of the class is in a corner of the room imitating yapping dogs. Another third are yowling cats, and the remaining third are in another corner as yelling children. After line 3 the yellow butterfly enters from the hallway or from behind something; it flies to each corner before delivering its lines.

❧ SUGGESTIONS FOR INTERPRETATION

There is much loud yapping, yowling, and yelling; they do not have to be in unison. The yellow butterfly should be very proud with huge imaginary wings. Before it flies away it should fly about the room several times before disappearing. Line 9 should be said softly with a touch of sadness.

❧ SUGGESTIONS FOR ENRICHMENT

The children can create some large yellow paper wings and go home as yellow butterflies.

Draw dogs with the word yap coming from their mouths, cats with the word yowl, and children with the word yell.

Everyone could try to wear something yellow one day.

Display different varieties of butterflies.

Yap, yowl, and yell

y

1. Dogs were **yapping** . . . yap, yap . . . yap, yap. (third the class)
2. Cats were **yowling** . . . yowl, yowl, yowl. (third the class)
3. Children were **yelling** . . . yell, yell . . . yell, yell, yell! (third the class)
4. Stop! said the **yellow** butterfly. (solo 1)
5. Why must you **yap**? (solo 1)
6. Why must you **yowl**? (solo 1)
7. Why must you **yell**? (solo 1)
8. **You'll** make my **yellow** wings fall off! (solo 1)
9. And the **yellow** butterfly flew away. (all)

ᘞᔦ REVIEW OF WORDS

yapping	yowl	you'll
yap	yelling	yellow
yowling	yell	

⋘§ SUGGESTIONS FOR STAGING

Solos 1 and 2 stand in front of the room each surrounded by chairs as if in individual cages. The race, of course, will be a walking race around the room.

⋘§ SUGGESTIONS FOR INTERPRETATION

Solos 1 and 2 should be encouraged to make all kinds of humorous facial expressions. The walking race should be in a slow definite rhythm. When the class joins in, the speed can increase guided by the teacher. Two children holding a string at a finish line would add to the excitement.

⋘§ SUGGESTIONS FOR ENRICHMENT

Draw zombies and zebras.

Construct a bulletin board covered with large green leaves. Children's cutouts of jungle animals as well as zebras and a few zombies could be interspersed among the leaves.

Discuss the feelings of a person winning and a person losing. What does one say to a winner? to a loser?

List other kinds of races: ski, toboggan, horse, and so on.

Make zombie masks of construction paper and items from the junk box.

Have some races on the playground: walking, running, three-legged, jumping, hopping, or a passing an apple under the chin race (inside on a rainy Friday afternoon).

Zoom, zoom!
zip, zip!

1. We saw a **zombie** at the **zoo**. (half the class)
2. His eyes were red, his lips were blue. (half the class)
3. The **zombie** said (half the class)
4. "**Zoom! Zoom!**" (solo 1)
5. We saw a **zebra** at the **zoo**. (other half)
6. His tail was green, his nose went kerchoo. (other half)
7. The **zebra** said (other half)
8. "**Zip! Zip!**" (solo 2)
9. And then the race began. (all)
10. **Zoom! Zoom!** (solo 1)
11. **Zip! Zip!** (solo 2)
12. **Ziggity! Ziggity!** (solo 1)
13. **Zappo!** (solo 2)
14. **Zoom! Zoom! Zip! Zip!** (all)
15. **Ziggity! Ziggity! Zappo!** (all)

REVIEW OF WORDS

zombie	zebra	ziggity
zoo	zip	zappo
zoom		

Section Two:
LONG AND SHORT VOWELS

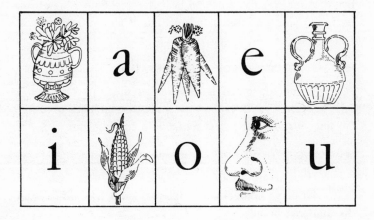

ᵕᓂ SUGGESTIONS FOR STAGING

Draw an apple tree with bright red apples on the board. Aunt Agatha can stand near the tree. Solo 1 stands up on line 5, and the class stands on line 8 and gathers around Aunt Agatha.

ᵕᓂ SUGGESTIONS FOR INTERPRETATION

Encourage much laughter from the class on lines 3 and 4. Aunt Agatha can wiggle and twist on lines 6 and 7. On lines 9 and 10 the class speaks in a coaxing tone.

ᵕᓂ SUGGESTIONS FOR ENRICHMENT

Have an apple party.

Display photographs of different aunts brought in from the children's homes.

Display pictures of different types of apples so children may identify them. Taste as many as possible.

Write a story from the ant's point of view. What did the ant see and do inside Aunt Agatha?

Put various words on apples for a paper tree attached to the bulletin board. Children can hang apples after identifying the words and giving their meanings.

*The ant
in my aunt*

1. The **ant** went in the **apple,** (half the class)
2. The big red **apple.** (other half)
3. Your **aunt** ate the **apple,** (half the class)
4. The big red **apple.** (other half)
5. Hey! The **ant** is in your **aunt!** (solo 1)
6. Ooooooh, I **can** feel **that ant!** (solo 2)
7. Ooooooh, I **can** feel **that ant!** (solo 2)
8. **Stand** still **Aunt Agatha! Stand** still! (all)
9. Come out little **ant!** (all)
10. Come out of my **aunt!** (all)

❧ REVIEW OF WORDS

ant	can	stand
apple	that	Agatha
aunt		

✑ SUGGESTIONS FOR STAGING

Line 1 is not delivered until the squirrel spots some acorns and begins eating. The same with lines 3 and 5. The squirrel, fish, and ape should be encouraged to use all parts of the room.

✑ SUGGESTIONS FOR INTERPRETATION

The squirrel is very frisky, the fish very wiggly, and the ape very ferocious. Find some way for the three animals to end up with dirty faces. For instance, they could hide behind something and smudge their faces with charcoal before presenting themselves to the class after line 9.

✑ SUGGESTIONS FOR ENRICHMENT

Make humorous drawings of messy faces.

Gather acorns.

Have a grape eating party.

Have three children hide pretend acorns (small pebbles) around the room while the other children cover their eyes so as not to see. They then turn into squirrels and have one minute to find as many acorns as they can.

Play the game squirrel in the trees. Two children hold hands to form a tree. Form several trees. The other children bounce about looking for acorns. They are then startled by a loud noise and run to a tree for safety. Of course, only so many will fit into a tree. Exchange places—trees become squirrels and squirrels become trees.

Messy, messy faces

1. The squirrel found some **acorns.** (all)
2. He **ate** and **ate** and **ate!** (solo 1)
3. The fish caught the **bait.** (all)
4. He **ate** and **ate** and **ate!** (solo 2)
5. The **ape** found a **grape.** (all)
6. He **ate** and **ate** and **ate!** (solo 3)
7. It was so **late** (all)
8. By the time they **ate** (all)
9. That they all went to bed (all)
10. With messy, messy **faces.** (all)

REVIEW OF WORDS

acorns	ape	late
ate	grape	faces
bait		

⇜§ SUGGESTIONS FOR STAGING

Half the class is in one corner of the room; the other half is in the opposite corner. The hen stands on top of a table representing mountain one; the echo is on top of a table representing mountain two. Seven children representing the seven eggs roll away from mountain one. When they hit the opposite wall, that will be the cue for line 12.

⇜§ SUGGESTIONS FOR INTERPRETATION

The echo should seem to come from far away. Lines 8, 9, and 10 should build up in volume and speed. Line 12 is extremely loud at the appropriate time. Lines 13 and 14 are very soft and sad.

⇜§ SUGGESTIONS FOR ENRICHMENT

Create a hen farm in which every child draws and labels a picture of a hen. Near each hen could be a collection of drawn eggs.

Locate all the items in the room that are empty.

Draw what an echo might look like.

Place vocabulary or number facts on drawn and cut-out eggs. To put an egg in an empty nest, children must give its correct meaning.

Teach the song "Little Sir Echo."

Raise a couple of baby chicks for a while.

Write or tape a story about how sad it is to be an echo and never have a chance to say anything first—always having to say what someone else has said.

*Seven
rolling
eggs*

e

1. On mountain one lived a **hen**. (half the class)
2. On mountain two lived an **echo**. (other half)
3. "**Hello**," said the little **hen**. (solo 1)
4. "**Hello**," answered the **echo**. (solo 2)
5. "I laid **seven eggs**," said the **hen**. (solo 1)
6. "I laid **seven eggs**," answered the **echo**. (solo 2)
7. Then the **eggs** began to roll. (all)
8. **Seven eggs** began to roll. (all)
9. **Seven eggs** began to roll. (all)
10. **Seven eggs** began to roll. (all)
11. The **echo yelled**, "Little **hen**, little **hen**, your **eggs** are rolling." (solo 2)
12. Crash! (all)
13. **Seven eggs** were smashed. (all)
14. The **nest** was **empty**. (all)

⮑ REVIEW OF WORDS

hen	seven	nest
echo	eggs	empty
hello	yelled	

◀§   SUGGESTIONS FOR STAGING

Line 1 all heads are on desks; line 2 everyone points up at the stars; line 3 everyone stands and points; line 4 one child stands on a chair and points; line 5 another child stands on a chair and points; line 6 all children stand on chairs and point; line 7 all heads on desks again; line 8 one child jumps up; line 9 everyone jumps up. At this point the children crumble up bits of paper to throw up to the stars to feed them. Line 10 half the class throws bits of paper upwards; line 11 the other half does the same; and line 12 everyone stands on chairs casting bits of paper up to the stars.

◀§   SUGGESTIONS FOR INTERPRETATION

Lines 1, 2, and 3 should be very soft; at line 4 excitement begins, line 5 more excitement, and line 6 very loud! Line 7 is very soft again, line 8 some excitement, and line 9 very loud. Encourage students to exaggerate the word *feed* and to hold the word as long as possible in lines 10, 11, and 12.

◀§   SUGGESTIONS FOR ENRICHMENT

Draw all different shapes and colored stars.

Place stars about the room asking children who can *see* a blue star, who can *see* a small star, who can *see* a big star, and so on.

Read some legends about the stars or the beliefs people held about them long ago.

Point out on a star chart some constellations such as the Big Dipper and Orion.

Ask the children to look in the sky at night and try to find the Big Dipper and other constellations.

Read poems about stars.

Write a cinquain about the stars and the heavens.

Feed the stars

1. It is **evening**. (all)
2. **See** the stars. (all)
3. **See** the beautiful stars. (all)
4. One million stars, (solo 1)
5. Two million stars, (solo 2)
6. **Three** million stars. (all)
7. It is **evening**. (all)
8. **Feed** the stars. (solo 3)
9. **Feed** the **three** million stars. (all)
10. **Feed**! (half the class)
11. **Feed**! (other half)
12. **Feed**! (all)

REVIEW OF WORDS

evening	three	feed
see		

◄§   SUGGESTIONS FOR STAGING

Solo 1 is in front of the room in much pain with a tummy ache. The class gathers around him on line 2. Solo 2 appears from out of sight carrying a large box on line 8. The children return to their seats on line 9.

◄§   SUGGESTIONS FOR INTERPRETATION

Solo 1 can exaggerate his pain, even pretending to cry! The class is very sympathetic and concerned at first but fairly disgusted on line 9. Solo 2 exclaims very loudly on line 8.

◄§   SUGGESTIONS FOR ENRICHMENT

Draw an immense box full of delicious candies.
Draw children ill in bed.
Discuss the word *immense* in the following manner:

    a.   A grasshopper looks immense to an ant.
    b.   A horse looks immense to a rabbit.
    c.   A giant looks immense to girls and boys.

Children can make other comparisons of their own.

I'm ill . . .
so ill!

i

1. Oh, I'm ill . . . so ill! (solo 1)
2. Why are you ill? (all)
3. What made you so ill? (all)
4. I don't know! I don't know! (solo 1)
5. Well, what **did** you eat? (all)
6. I ate some **fish**! (solo 1)
7. That wouldn't make you ill! (all)
8. He ate all the candy **in this immense** box! (solo 2)
9. Now we know what made you ill! (all)

❧ REVIEW OF WORDS

ill	fish	this
did	in	immense

❧ SUGGESTIONS FOR STAGING

Solo 1 should stand on a chair or a table against the blackboard. On line 1 half the class go close to the icy icicle and then return to their seats. On line 2 the other half go up, observe the icicle, and then return to their seats. On line 5 the class stands.

❧ SUGGESTIONS FOR INTERPRETATION

Solo 1 is very frightened as she or he begins to melt, crying out on lines 6 and 7. On line 8 the class crouch on the floor near their desks, on line 9 they stand, on line 10 they stand on their chairs, and on line 11 they stand on their desks. Each line gets progressively louder and louder and hotter and hotter. Arms are fully extended on line 11, send out hot sun rays. All during this the icy icicle is melting and melting and after line 11 becomes a pool of water on the floor. Solo 2 goes up to the melted icy icicle and sadly delivers the final line.

❧ SUGGESTIONS FOR ENRICHMENT

Draw huge icy icicles.

Discuss how different things look in sunlight and in moonlight.

Divide the class into four sections. Place four icy ice cubes into four separate dishes. See which ice cube melts first. The children can blow hot air on the ice cubes so that their cube will melt faster and win the race.

The icy icicle **i**

1. The **icy icicle** is long, so long. (half the class)
2. The **icy icicle** is smooth, so smooth. (other half)
3. It **shines** in the **moonlight**! (half the class)
4. It **shines** in the **sunlight**! (other half)
5. Oh, oh! It's beginning to melt! (all)
6. My **ice** is turning to water! (solo 1)
7. Oh, no! My **ice** is turning to water!!! (solo 1)
8. It was noon and the sun began to **shine**, (all)
9. And **shine**! (all)
10. And **Shine**!! (all)
11. **AND SHINE**!!! (all)
12. And the **icy icicle** was no more. (solo 2)

🦢 REVIEW OF WORDS

icy	moonlight	ice
icicle	sunlight	shine
shines		

~§ SUGGESTIONS FOR STAGING

Mom, solo 3, stays out of sight and appears only on lines 4 and 11. The class stands and speaks in an annoyed tone on line 6.

~§ SUGGESTIONS FOR INTERPRETATION

Tom and Bob, solos 1 and 2, call very loudly to Mom and are very impatient! On lines 6 and 7 the class surround solos 1 and 2, scold them, and then return to their seats.

~§ SUGGESTIONS FOR ENRICHMENT

Draw mothers.

Draw hot things.

Have children bring in labels from cans of soup to start a classroom soup store!

Warm up some alphabet soup on a hot plate and give every child a cupful. He or she must identify the letters of the alphabet in his or her cup before eating them.

Read *Chicken Soup with Rice* by Maurice Sendak (Harper & Row, 1962; pap., Scholastic Book Services, 1970).

Is the soup on, mom?

O

1. **Mom!** Hey, **Mom!** (solos 1 and 2)
2. Yes, **Tom.** Yes, **Bob.** (solo 3)
3. **Mom,** is the soup **on, Mom?** (solos 1 and 2)
4. **Not** yet, **Tom. Not** yet, **Bob.** (solo 3)
5. But **Mom,** it's taking so long! (solos 1 and 2)
6. **Now** stop it! **Stop** it! (class)
7. Your **Mom** is busy with **other** chores. (class)
8. **Mom!** Hey, **Mom!** (solos 1 and 2)
9. Yes, **Tom.** Yes, **Bob.** (solo 3)
10. **Mom,** is the soup **on, Mom?** (solos 1 and 2)
11. Soup is **hot! Come** and get it! (solo 3)
12. And they all lived happily ever after! (class)

ﺮ§ REVIEW OF WORDS

Mom	not	other
Tom	now	hot
Bob	stop	come
on		

ᴇᢒ SUGGESTIONS FOR STAGING

Solos 1, 2, 3, 4, and 5 are in imaginary beds in the front or center of the room. The class have their heads on their desks attempting to get some rest. Everyone stands on line 10.

ᴇᢒ SUGGESTIONS FOR INTERPRETATION

Solos 1, 2, 3, 4, and 5 can pretend to be little children who are restless. The children are patient until lines 10 and 11, when they become irritated.

ᴇᢒ SUGGESTIONS FOR ENRICHMENT

Make a list of what happens to various parts of the body when one has a cold, for example, my nose runs, gets red, is stuffed up, and the like.

Write a letter (class composed and teacher scribed) to someone who is sick—a friend or an old person.

Discuss ways of making someone who is sick feel better.

Discuss the meaning of the word impatient and what makes people—themselves as well as their parents—become impatient.

Let the children compile a list of things that makes their teacher impatient.

Go to sleep

O

1. I'm **cold**! I'm **cold**! (solo 1)
2. Stop **moaning**! Stop **moaning**! (all)
3. Get my **robe**! Get my **robe**! (solo 2)
4. Stop **moaning**! Stop **moaning**! (all)
5. My **throat**! My **throat**! (solo 3)
6. Stop **moaning**! Stop **moaning**! (all)
7. My **nose**! My **nose**! (solo 4)
8. Stop **moaning**! Stop **moaning**! (all)
9. I have a **cold**! A terrible **cold**! (solo 5)
10. Stop **moaning** and **groaning**! (all)
11. And **go** to sleep! (all)

∽ʓ REVIEW OF WORDS

cold	throat	groaning
moaning	nose	go
robe		

◆§ SUGGESTIONS FOR STAGING

A turned over table at the front of the room can be the tub. Solos 1 and 2 can huddle in a far corner of the room.

◆§ SUGGESTIONS FOR INTERPRETATION

The class is very calm and composed at the beginning and becomes increasingly annoyed at each sequence. On lines 1, 5, and 9 everyone points to the tub. On line 13 the class stands and loudly issues a command that cannot be ignored by solos 1 and 2.

◆§ SUGGESTIONS FOR ENRICHMENT

Draw tubs with children or silly things such as an elephant, horse, or monster in them.

Write a story telling what children take into the bathtub with them.

Pantomime taking a bath.

Make a big tub on the bulletin board and let children make cutouts of themselves to put into the tub. Include favorite toy cutouts too. The title might be "Rub-a-dub-dub, 20 children in a tub!"

*Get in that tub
and scrub!*

u

1. Time for a bath. (all)
2. **Jump** in the **tub** (all)
3. And **scrub, scrub, scrub!** (all)
4. No, thank you! No **tub** for **us!** (solos 1 and 2)
5. Time for a bath. (all)
6. Take the **brush** (all)
7. And **rub, rub, rub!** (all)
8. No, thank you. No **tub** for **us!** (solos 1 and 2)
9. Time for a bath! (all)
10. Take your **duck** (all)
11. And get off that **smudge!** (all)
12. No, thank you. No **tub** for **us!** (solos 1 and 2)
13. Get in that **tub** and scrub! (all)

⋙ REVIEW OF WORDS

jump	us	duck
tub	brush	smudge
scrub	rub	

ᴥᶘ SUGGESTIONS FOR STAGING

Solos 1, 2, and 3 should pop out from various sections of the room when they make their statements and pop away when finished. On lines 2, 5, and 8 the class should stand when asking their questions. After line 9 everyone should go to the window and look thoughtfully out as they finish their lines.

ᴥᶘ SUGGESTIONS FOR INTERPRETATION

Solos 1, 2, and 3 should be very emphatic about their statements. On lines 2, 5, and 8 the class should forcefully question the truth of each statement. At the window, the class should speak their lines in a dreamy manner.

ᴥᶘ SUGGESTIONS FOR ENRICHMENT

Paint a large mural with a large mule, a large prune, and a large plume. The class can decide what favorite tune to sing.

Make plumes from construction paper to wear for a while.

Make a list of phrases telling how it would feel to ride a mule.

Make flutes out of clay or straws. While wearing their plumes and playing their flutes, the children can take turns riding on each other's back.

Is that true?
really true?

u

1. Some **mules** eat **prunes**! (solo 1)
2. Is that **true**? Really **true**? (all)
3. It's **true**! It's **true**! (solo 1)
4. Some **mules** wear **plumes**! (solo 2)
5. It that **true**? Really **true**? (all)
6. It's **true**! It's **true**! (solo 2)
7. Some **mules** play **flutes**! (solo 3)
8. Is that **true**? Really **true**? (all)
9. It's **true**! It's **true**! (solo 3)
10. I wonder, I wonder, (all)
11. How it would feel (all)
12. To ride on a **mule** (all)
13. Who was wearing a **plume** (all)
14. And eating a **prune** (all)
15. While playing our favorite **tune**? (all)

✍ REVIEW OF WORDS

mules	true	flutes
prunes	plumes	tune

Section Three:
BLENDS

bl		cl	fl	gl
	pl	sl	sp	ar
br	cr	dr	fr	gr
pr	tr	st		sw
tw	scr		spl	str

⇜ SUGGESTIONS FOR STAGING

Solo 2 is in bed (on a table), head on pillow, covered by a blue blanket and sound asleep. Solo 1 starts out in the hallway or in a corner of the room.

⇜ SUGGESTIONS FOR INTERPRETATION

On line 1 the class points to the sky, on line 3 it points to a specific part of the room, on line 5 it points to an area close to the bed, and, of course, on line 7 it points to the blue blanket. Solo 1 flies about the room becoming louder and louder and louder. She or he grabs the blue blanket after line 8 and runs away. Solo 2 awakens and shivers and shivers and is very sad on line 12.

⇜ SUGGESTIONS FOR ENRICHMENT

Draw pictures of the power of the wind.

Listen to a record with wind sounds.

Compose a story about where the blue blanket went and what happened to it.

Read a story about a storm, for instance, *Time of Wonder* by Robert McCloskey (Viking Press, 1957).

Draw a large tree and have children put multicolored blossoms all over it.

Blowing cold!
blowing colder! **bl**

1. A **black** sky, a **blowing** wind! (all)
2. **Blowing** cold! **Blowing** colder! (solo 1)
3. A tree of **blossoms**, a **blowing** wind! (all)
4. **Blowing** cold! **Blowing** colder! (solo 1)
5. A kitchen door, a **blowing** wind! (all)
6. **Blowing** cold! **Blowing** colder! (solo 1)
7. A **blue blanket**, a **blowing** wind! (all)
8. **Blowing** cold! **Blowing** colder! (solo 1)
9. Out the kitchen door! (third of class)
10. Over the **blossoms**! (another third of class)
11. Into the **black** sky! (last third of class)
12. And I never saw my **blue blanket** again! (solo 2)

◆§ REVIEW OF WORDS

black	blossoms	blanket
blowing	blue	

✧ SUGGESTIONS FOR STAGING

A custodian can provide a small ladder. If the children are too young to pretend falling down, a raggedy clown doll could be attached to the end of a stick so that the child never leaves the floor. Half the class should be on one side of the ladder and the other half on the other side.

✧ SUGGESTIONS FOR INTERPRETATION

The rhythm of the class will go fast, medium, or slow according to the person manipulating the clown. Be very loud on line 9.

✧ SUGGESTIONS FOR ENRICHMENT

Draw all types of clowns.

Collect pictures of clowns.

Have a clown day during which everyone dresses up as a clown, including the teacher.

Discuss the actions of clowns seen at circuses and parades.

Make clown puppets out of old socks and scraps.

The clumsy clown cl

1. Up the ladder **climbed** the **clown** (half the class)
2. To **clean** the **closet** shelf. (half the class)
3. Up the ladder **climbed** the **clown**. (other half)
4. He **climbed** and **climbed** and **climbed**. (other half)
5. Down the ladder fell the **clown**. (half the class)
6. The **clumsy clown**, the **clumsy clown**. (half the class)
7. Down the ladder fell the **clown**. (other half)
8. **Clippity clop! Clippity clop!** (other half)
9. **CLUMP!** (all)

❧ REVIEW OF WORDS

climbed	closet	clop
clown	clumsy	clump
clean	clippity	

ี SUGGESTIONS FOR STAGING

The flower, the cornflake, and the flapjack are stationed in three different areas of the room. Solo 1 is a large bird, spreading his huge wings while flying about the room.

ี SUGGESTIONS FOR INTERPRETATION

Solo 1 flies all about the room and hovers over solos 2, 3, and 4. The class is annoyed that solo 1 doesn't realize that solos 2, 3, and 4 can't fly. When solos 2, 3, and 4 decide they can fly, they do so by grabbing the extended arms of solo 1 and hold on and run about the room with him. Line 19 should be soft and fade away.

ี SUGGESTIONS FOR ENRICHMENT

Draw large birds with huge wings.

Eat some dry cornflakes.

Make a big butterfly for the bulletin board. Use old pieces of nylon or other filmy material for the wings.

Write words or number facts on flowers or flapjacks. These can be placed on the butterfly for a ride, if the meaning or the fact is known.

Fly with me

fl

1. **Fly** with me, **fly** away! (solo 1)
2. **Fly**, **fly** away! (solo 1)
3. I can't **fly**! I'm a **flower**! (solo 2)
4. Just a little **flower**! (solo 2)
5. She can't **fly**, she's a **flower**! (all)
6. **Fly** with me, **fly** away! (solo 1)
7. **Fly**, **fly** away! (solo 1)
8. I can't **fly**! I'm a cornflake! (solo 3)
9. A little crunchy cornflake! (solo 3)
10. She can't **fly**, she's a cornflake! (all)
11. **Fly** with me, **fly** away! (solo 1)
12. **Fly**, **fly** away! (solo 1)
13. I can't **fly**! I'm a **flapjack**! (solo 4)
14. A roly-poly **flapjack**! (solo 4)
15. He can't **fly**, he's a **flapjack**! (all)
16. Grab my wings and you will **fly**! (solo 1)
17. Look at them **fly** way up high! (all)
18. Look at them **fly** into the sky! (all)
19. Look at them **fly** away, away, away. (all)

REVIEW OF WORDS

fly	cornflake	flapjack
flower		

ᴥ§   SUGGESTIONS FOR STAGING

Solos 2 and 3 are lined up ready to go skating. The desks or tables are pushed together so that they can skate in a big, well-defined circle. They begin to skate after line 1. On line 5 solo 2 jumps on a table to make his announcement. Solos 3 and 4 begin to skate as they say lines 6 and 7. As they disappear into a closet or hallway, one skater drops a glove. Solo 5 says line 8 and skates after them.

ᴥ§   SUGGESTIONS FOR INTERPRETATION

The class says lines 2, 3, and 4 in a steady rhythmical fashion. Solo 2 is very excited on line 5. Speak lines 6 and 7 in a steady skating rhythm.

ᴥ§   SUGGESTIONS FOR ENRICHMENT

Draw skaters doing fantastic feats.

Make dioramas of skating scenes. Dress figures (made of clay) in real clothes using scraps of material from the junk box.

Play "The Skaters' Waltz" and pretend to skate.

Place a large mirror flat on a table. Make skating figures to place on it. Put trees and shrubs and cotton round it to make a winter scene.

*Get ready,
get set, go!*

gl

1. Get ready, get set, go! (solo 1)
2. **Gliding, gliding** over the ice. (all)
3. **Gliding, gliding** over the **glistening** ice. (all)
4. **Gliding, gliding** over the **glassy** ice. (all)
5. Look up! Look up! The stars are **glittering**. (solo 2)
6. Our faces are **glowing**. (solos 3 and 4)
7. As we **glide, glide, glide** away. (solos 3 and 4)
8. Hey! You dropped your **glove**! (solo 5)

REVIEW OF WORDS

gliding	glittering	glide
glistening	glowing	glove
glassy		

◄ℰ SUGGESTIONS FOR STAGING

Solos 1, 2, and 3 hide out of sight so the class hears only the sounds. Solo 4 stands on line 7. Class stands after line 7.

◄ℰ SUGGESTIONS FOR INTERPRETATION

On line 1 solos 1, 2, and 3 should be soft, increasing in volume on line 3 and becoming very loud on line 5. If the class chooses, it can repeat the last four lines.

◄ℰ SUGGESTIONS FOR ENRICHMENT

Invite the principal in to hear the banjo recital.

Listen to a recording of a banjo.

Find a community person who plays the banjo, invite him or her in, and have a song-fest. You might invite the class next door to come too.

Plinkity!
plinkity!
plink!

pl

1. **Plinkity, plinkity, plink!** (solos 1, 2, and 3)
2. What's that sound we hear? (all)
3. **Plinkity, plinkity, plink!** (solos 1, 2, and 3)
4. We've heard that sound before. (all)
5. **Plinkity, plinkity, plink!** (solos 1, 2, and 3)
6. It's a banjo sound, of course! (all)
7. Pick up your banjos and we'll **play** the teacher a tune!
   (solo 4)
8. **Plinkity, plinkity, plink!** (all)
9. **Plinkity, plinkity, plank!** (all)
10. **Plinkity, plinkity, plink!** (all)
11. **Plinkity, plinkity, plunk!** (all)

❧ REVIEW OF WORDS

plinkity	play	plunk
plink	plank	

◆§ SUGGESTIONS FOR STAGING

Solo 4 is in front of the room as a pretend driver of a make-believe car. Sitting in a chair holding an imaginary wheel will suffice. As the class and solos 1, 2, and 3 deliver each command, they should stand up when beginning and sit down when finished.

◆§ SUGGESTIONS FOR INTERPRETATION

The class and solos 1, 2, and 3 should speak with very anxious, worried voices.

◆§ SUGGESTIONS FOR ENRICHMENT

Draw road signs including a DRIVE SLOWLY one.

Discuss the weather and what makes roads icy and slippery.

Draw a car sliding on a road and add snow by using chalk.

If it is winter and in a cold climate, discuss safety rules for sleds, skates, skis, and the like.

Drive slowly s**l**

1. Drive **slowly**, the road is **slippery**! (half the class)
2. Drive **slowly**, the ice has turned to **slush**! (other half)
3. Look out for that **sled**! (solo 1)
4. Look out for that **slab** of stone! (solo 2)
5. Don't **slam** on the brakes! (solo 3)
6. We don't want the car to **slide**! (all)
7. Stop it! You're making me nervous! (solo 4)

❦ REVIEW OF WORDS

slowly	sled	slam
slippery	slab	slide
slush		

◄§   SUGGESTIONS FOR STAGING

A child representing the spider can draw a web on the blackboard, and when it is completed, the class begins its lines. After line 2 solo 1 flies by the web. After line 6 the fly speeds by again.

◄§   SUGGESTIONS FOR INTERPRETATION

The class presents the lines very softly and quietly. Lines 2, 4, and 6 should be slow and deliberate. Line 9 should be extremely slow. In line 7 solo 1 should be happy and care-free, flying about the room.

◄§   SUGGESTIONS FOR ENRICHMENT

Draw all kinds of spooky spiders.

Children can look for pictures of spiders at home.

Find a real live spider for the children to observe.

Look for books about spiders and examine detailed photographs or drawings of spider webs and various spiders.

Sing the "Eency Weency Spider" song.

Read some African folktales about Anansi the Spider such as those by Gerald McDermott (Holt, 1973), Peggy Appiah (Pantheon, 1966) or Philip K. Sherlock (T. Y. Crowell, 1954).

The spooky spider **sp**

1. A **spooky spider spun** a web. (all)
2. He waited, waited, waited. (all)
3. He **spied** a fly go **speeding** by. (all)
4. He waited, waited, waited. (all)
5. The **spider** didn't **speak** a word. (all)
6. He waited, waited, waited. (all)
7. Zip went the fly, right on by! (solo 1)
8. And there sat the **spider**. (all)
9. Waiting, waiting, waiting. (all)

₰ REVIEW OF WORDS

spooky	spun	speeding
spider	spied	speak

◆§ SUGGESTIONS FOR STAGING

Half the class faces the front wall, the other half of class faces the back wall. They do not see each other!

◆§ SUGGESTIONS FOR INTERPRETATION

Each group should make their voices sound as if they are far, far away—a touch of an echo or hollow sound.

◆§ SUGGESTIONS FOR ENRICHMENT

Discuss what is far, far away.

Draw stars.

Make cards to send to distant friends or relatives.

List real places where a person could be far from the classroom.

List the three wishes each child would make on a star.

Describe how it would feel to hold a star in one's hands.

*A card
from far away*

ar

1. We sent you a **card** from **far, far** away, (half the class)
2. From **far, far** away. (half the class)
3. We sent you a **card** from **far, far** away, (half the class)
4. Wondering how you **are** today. (half the class)
5. We sent you a **card** from **far, far** away, (other half)
6. From **far, far** away. (other half)
7. We sent you a **card** from **far, far** away, (other half)
8. Wondering how you **are** today. (other half)
9. We wished on a **star** from **far, far** away (half the class)
10. That you were here with us today. (half the class)
11. We wished on a **star** from **far, far** away (other half)
12. That you'd come back again someday. (other half)

✑ REVIEW OF WORDS

card	are	star
far		

SUGGESTIONS FOR STAGING

Place a table in front of the room where solos 1 and 2 can sit.

SUGGESTIONS FOR INTERPRETATION

On lines 1, 2, 3, and 4 the class calls as if Brenda and Bruce are far away. On line 5 solo 1 stands up and then sits; on line 7 solo 2 stands up and then sits. Solos 3 and 4 come rushing in after line 8 and exclaim very loudly on line 11.

SUGGESTIONS FOR ENRICHMENT

Draw a big loaf of brown bread and a big bowl of bran flakes—and some delicious brownies!

Give a brownie party prepared by the teacher or parents.

Make a list of all kinds of breakfast foods.

Eat some bran flakes.

Compile a list of words describing how brownies taste, i.e., scrumptious, delicious, and so on.

Munch,
munch,
smack, munch

br

1. It's **breakfast** time! (all)
2. **Brenda**! **Brenda**! Come and get your **breakfast**. (all)
3. It's **breakfast** time! (all)
4. **Bruce**! **Bruce**! Come and get your **breakfast**. (all)
5. I am some **bran** flakes. (solo 1)
6. Come and eat me! (solo 1)
7. I am some **brown bread**. (solo 2)
8. Come and eat me! (solo 2)
9. SO! **Brenda** and **Bruce** ate the **bran** flakes. (all)
10. And **Brenda** and **Bruce** ate the **brown bread**. (all)
11. Munch! Munch! Smack! Munch! (solos 3 and 4)

◄§ REVIEW OF WORDS

breakfast	Bruce	brown
Brenda	bran	bread

❧ SUGGESTIONS FOR STAGING

The student playing solo 2 should actually creep and crawl about the room. The cricket, solo 3, should be on a table watching. He exerts much effort to get the creeping, crawling creeper out of the crack.

❧ SUGGESTIONS FOR INTERPRETATION

The class should whisper the lines so as not to frighten the creeper. Solo 2 says line 7 with much fear and anguish.

❧ SUGGESTIONS FOR ENRICHMENT

Draw crickets and cracks.

If possible go on a cricket hunt.

Listen to a record of cricket sounds. List some ideas about what was creeping and crawling and write stories about it. If the weather is warm, ask children to listen for cricket sounds at night. Look at drawings of crickets and learn something about their habits.

Introduce children to the Walt Disney character Jiminy Cricket.

Read *The Cricket in Times Square* by George Selden (Farrar Straus, 1960).

*It fell
into a crack* **cr**

1. It is **creeping, creeping, creeping.** (half the class)
2. It is **crawling, crawling, crawling** (other half)
3. **Across** our garden floor. (all)
4. It **creeps!** (all)
5. It **crawls!** (all)
6. Look! It has fallen into a **crack!** (solo 1)
7. "Help me! Help me!" it **cried!** (solo 2)
8. "I'll help you," said the **cricket.** (solo 3)
9. And then it went **creeping** and **crawling** away. (all)

〜§ REVIEW OF WORDS

creeping	creeps	cried
crawling	crawls	cricket
across	crack	

ᴥᶫ   SUGGESTIONS FOR STAGING

The two raindrops, solos 1 and 2, should be standing on a table. The lady dragon is asleep in another part of the room.

ᴥᶫ   SUGGESTIONS FOR INTERPRETATION

The two raindrops should make their dripping sound emphatic and distinct. The lady dragon, solo 3, can be as ferocious as she wishes. She might wear an old evening gown and even a fancy hat. The class can imitate motor noises as the lady dragon drives her car down the drive. When she reaches the raindrops, she should gobble them up!

ᴥᶫ   SUGGESTIONS FOR ENRICHMENT

Draw a lady dragon in a dragon car or raindrops.

Perhaps eat some tasty gumdrops.

Read the story *The Dragon's Handbook* by Barbara Rinkoff (Nelson, 1966; pap., Scholastic Book Services).

The lady dragon # dr

1. **Drip, drop! Drip, drop!** (solos 1 and 2)
2. The lady **dragon** awoke from her **dream.** (all)
3. **Drip, drop! Drip, drop!** (solos 1 and 2)
4. I hear some water **dripping.** (solo 3)
5. **Drip, drop! Drip, drop!** (solos 1 and 2)
6. My throat is **dry!** (solo 3)
7. **Drip, drop! Drip, drop!** (solos 1 and 2)
8. I must get a **drink.** (solo 3)
9. She put on her **dress,** (all)
10. **Drove** down the **drive,** (all)
11. And **drank** every **drop** that was **dripping!** (all)

~§ REVIEW OF WORDS

drip	dripping	drove
drop	dry	drive
dragon	drink	drank
dream	dress	

~§ SUGGESTIONS FOR STAGING

Solo 1 is the mother standing in the front of the room near a large table. Underneath the cooking table are five or six children representing solo 2 as the French fries. After line 5 the mother puts the French fries on the cooking table. On lines 8, 9, 10, 13, 14, and 15 the French fries are bouncing about on the table as they say their lines. On line 17 the class gathers about the cooking table to "eat" the French fries.

~§ SUGGESTIONS FOR INTERPRETATION

Solo 1 could wear an apron and hold a fork, spoon, or spatula. Children playing the part of solo 2 should create the feeling that they are cooking—a pleasant cooking feeling. Each frizzle, frazzle should get louder and louder with line 15 hitting a magnificent crescendo!

~§ SUGGESTIONS FOR ENRICHMENT

Draw pictures of things the children have seen being fried at home or on TV.

Be a French fry frizzling in a pan, and tape record how you feel and tell what's happening to you.

Make a list of foods mothers fry.

Go to a McDonald's and eat some French fries while on a field trip.

Let the children keep a box as a pretend pan. Cut strips of paper to look like French fries and write favorite words on them. When a child knows a word and has used it in a story two times, he may color his French fry brown and put it in his pan for good.

Frizzle,
frazzle
in the pan

1. What's for dinner, Mom? (all)
2. **French fries!** (solo 1)
3. **French fries!** (solo 1)
4. **Fry** the **French fries**, Mom! (all)
5. **Fry** them! **Fry** them! **Fry** them! (all)
6. Listen to them **fry!** (solo 1)
7. Listen to them **fry!** (solo 1)
8. **Frizzle, frazzle** in the pan. (solo 2)
9. **Frizzle, frazzle** in the pan. (solo 2)
10. **Frizzle, frazzle** in the pan. (solo 2)
11. Listen to them **fry!** (solo 1)
12. Listen to them **fry!** (solo 1)
13. **Frizzle, frazzle** in the pan. (solo 2)
14. **Frizzle, frazzle** in the pan. (solo 2)
15. **Frizzle, frazzle** in the pan. (solo 2)
16. They're done! (solo 1)
17. Hooray! Let's eat the **French fries!** (all)

◦§ REVIEW OF WORDS

French	fry	frazzle
fries	frizzle	

⋅◈ SUGGESTIONS FOR STAGING

The big, green-eyed groundhog should be out of sight while groaning and growling. On line 5 the class begins to become afraid, and on line 7 everyone scampers into a corner of the room to get away. Grandfather and grandmother come out of an imaginary house to investigate the noise.

⋅◈ SUGGESTIONS FOR INTERPRETATION

Grandfather and grandmother are not afraid of the noises. The green-eyed groundhog could have green circles around his eyes and attempt to scare the children.

⋅◈ SUGGESTIONS FOR ENRICHMENT

Tell stories about grandmothers and grandfathers.

Finish stories about what happened *after* the green-eyed groundhog came out of the tall grass.

Paint pictures of the green-eyed groundhog or green-eyed monsters, cover paintings with strips of green construction paper to make them hide in the grass.

Great green eyes gr

1. The **green grass** began to **grow**. (all)
2. It **grew** and **grew** and **grew**! (all)
3. Oh, how it **grew**! (solo 1)
4. Something **groaned** in that tall **green grass**. (all)
5. It **groaned**, and **groaned**, and **groaned**! (all)
6. Oh, how it **groaned**! (solo 2)
7. Something **growled** in that tall **green grass**. (all)
8. It **growled**, and **growled**, and **growled**! (all)
9. "What's that **groaning** in the **grass**?" **grumbled grandfather**. (solo 3)
10. "What's that **growling** in the **grass**?" **grumbled grandmother**. (solo 4)
11. Then out from the tall **green grass** came a **great** big **green**-eyed **groundhog**! (all)

❧ REVIEW OF WORDS

green	growled	growling
grass	groaning	grandmother
grow	grumbled	great
grew	grandfather	groundhog
groaned		

꿍 SUGGESTIONS FOR STAGING

When the prince and princess enter, they should go to a chair or stepladder that will enable them to climb easily onto a table where they stand above everyone. The six trumpeters can be in the back of the room, near the door through which the prince and princess enter or out of sight. After line 8 the class should kneel in front of the prince and princess. Ask for two volunteers to be the prince and princess.

꿍 SUGGESTIONS FOR INTERPRETATION

The prince and princess should be very regal and wear capes and crowns, if possible. The trumpeters exclaim very loudly and in unison. As the royalty leaves, the class waves good-bye.

꿍 SUGGESTIONS FOR ENRICHMENT

Make paper or cardboard crowns.

Read some fairy tales and discuss what happens to the princes and princesses.

Read stories such as "The Princess and the Pea," "Sleeping Beauty," or "The Frog Prince."

Discuss what a promise means, what promises the children have made, and the importance of not breaking promises.

*The prince
and princess*

pr

1. Da-da! Da-da! Da-da! (six students)
2. Here comes the **prince**! (all)
3. Da-da! Da-da! Da-da! (same six students)
4. Here comes the **princess**! (all)
5. Da-da! Da-da! Da-da! (same six students)
6. There stands the **prince**! (all)
7. Da-da! Da-da! Da-da! (same six students)
8. There stands the **princess**! (all)
9. And they gave each other a **present**. (solo 1)
10. The **present** was a **promise**. (all)
11. **A promise** to love each other for evermore! (all)
12. Da-da! Da-da! Da-da! (same six students)
13. There go the **prince** and **princess**! (all)

᪨ REVIEW OF WORDS

prince	present	promise
princess		

SUGGESTIONS FOR STAGING

Divide the class in half. One half of the class stands against the front wall; the other half against the back wall. On lines 3, 4, 5, and 6 the children jump forward. On line 7 both halves make a big circle. On line 8, solo 1 jumps into the center of the circle to make his or her announcement.

SUGGESTIONS FOR INTERPRETATION

Beginning with line 3, each line should be spoken louder and louder. Line 7 should be the loudest!

SUGGESTIONS FOR ENRICHMENT

Draw trucks, trolleys, trains, traffic jams, and the like. Draw a trampoline with a child bouncing high on it.

Have children bring in small trucks and trains. Create a table display of city living with apartments, bridges, and tracks. Children could create and solve traffic jams.

*I'd rather be
a boy or
a girl*

tr

1. **Trucks** and **traffic** have to stay on streets. (half the class)
2. **Trolleys** and **trains** have to stay on **tracks**. (other half)
3. But boys and girls can run down **trails**, (half the class)
4. And climb up **trees**, (other half)
5. And play on **trumpets**, (half the class)
6. And jump on **trampolines**! (other half)
7. We can **try** almost anything! (all)
8. I'd rather be a boy or girl than a **trolley**, a **train**, or a **truck**. (solo 1)

👒 REVIEW OF WORDS

trucks	tracks	trumpets
traffic	trails	trampolines
trolleys	trees	try
trains		

⊷§   SUGGESTIONS FOR STAGING

Solos 1, 2, 3, and 4 stand in front of the class.

⊷§   SUGGESTIONS FOR INTERPRETATION

As the solos present their lines, they should be encouraged to act out their individual problems. On line 9 the class stands and points to the stumble trouble, then to the still trouble, then to the step trouble, and finally the stuck trouble. After line 9 the class forms a circle around the four troubles and loudly says line 10.

⊷§   SUGGESTIONS FOR ENRICHMENT

Draw each trouble and discuss these experiences.

Discuss what mothers would do and say when a child had one of these troubles.

Make a list of things (other than these) that are troubles for children.

Have a group prepare a puppet show with one of these troubles, i.e., gum in the hair, as the main theme.

Trouble, trouble, trouble!

st

1. I **stumbled**! (solo 1)
2. Bump! Bump! Bump! (all)
3. I can't sit **still**! (solo 2)
4. Wiggle! Wiggle! Wiggle! (all)
5. I **stepped** in a puddle! (solo 3)
6. Wet! Wet! Wet! (all)
7. I **stuck** gum in my hair! (solo 4)
8. Ouch! Ouch! Ouch! (all)
9. **Stumble! Still! Step! Stuck!** (all)
10. Oh, what troubles! (all)

❧ REVIEW OF WORDS

stumbled	stepped	stumble
still	stuck	

SUGGESTIONS FOR STAGING

The six swans will crouch and walk on their feet pretending they are swimming. As the lines progress, they swim from the front of the room to the back and back to the front. On line 7 the children stand on their chairs, jump into the water, and swim after the swans. Of course, they swim differently from the swans. They can stand up and move their arms or lie on their tummies and pretend they are swimming.

SUGGESTIONS FOR INTERPRETATION

When the six swans are swimming, they should stay close together as a group. On line 10 the six swans could swim right out of the classroom into the hallway, disappearing from sight.

SUGGESTIONS FOR ENRICHMENT

Draw swans in a lake.

Tell the class the story of *Swan Lake.*

Play some of the music from Tchaikovsky's *Swan Lake* after telling the story.

Let children dance (with toe shoes if they have them) or draw pictures they thought of while listening to the music.

Read the story *The Ugly Duckling* by Hans Christian Andersen. Draw before and after pictures of the ugly duckling and beautiful swan.

*Six
swimming
swans* SW

1. Down the river **swam** six **swans**. (all)
2. **Swimming, swimming, swimming.** (six swans)
3. They made the water **swish** and **swirl**. (all)
4. **Swimming, swimming, swimming.** (six swans)
5. They **swam** to shore and **swept** out again. (all)
6. **Swimming, swimming, swimming.** (six swans)
7. And we went after them. (all)
8. **Swimming, swimming, swimming!** (all)
9. But they **swiftly swam** away. (all)
10. **Swimming, swimming, swimming.** (six swans)

❧ REVIEW OF WORDS

swam	swish	swept
swans	swirl	swiftly
swimming		

⋙ SUGGESTIONS FOR STAGING

The twelve birds huddle close together on a table. On line 7 two students go to the table and pretend to give it a shake. The class stands on line 9, and the birds fall off the table.

⋙ SUGGESTIONS FOR INTERPRETATION

The twittering of the birds should be very sweet and joyful. They do not have to be in unison. On line 9 the class shouts a very loud SNAP. After the birds have fallen to the floor, their twittering on line 12 is very sad and tearful.

⋙ SUGGESTIONS FOR ENRICHMENT

Draw a long branch with twelve twittering birds.

Listen to a record of bird songs.

Discuss the care of birds in the home and how birds care for themselves if they are free.

Learn about nest building and the habits of some common birds in the area.

Go on a bird walk and try to see some birds indigenous to the area.

Collect and display bird pictures.

Contact the Aubudon Society for a representative to come to class and tell about birds.

Have a bird day and allow anyone who can to bring a bird and cage to school.

Twitter, twitter, twitter

tw

1. **Twelve** birds on a **twig**. (all)
2. **Twitter, twitter, twitter.** (solos 1-12)
3. **Twice** we told them the **twig** will break. (all)
4. **Twitter, twitter, twitter.** (solos 1-12)
5. **Twilight** came, and there they **twittered**. (all)
6. **Twitter, twitter, twitter.** (solos 1-12)
7. We gave the **twig** a **twist**. (all)
8. **Twitter, twitter, twitter.** (solos 1-12)
9. Then, SNAP went the **twig**. (all)
10. **Twitter, twitter, twitter.** (solos 1-12)

> REVIEW OF WORDS

twelve	twitter	twilight
twig	twice	twist

୶ᢒ   SUGGESTIONS FOR STAGING

Solos 1, 2, and 3 sit at their desks or tables with the class. Solo 4 is out of sight.

୶ᢒ   SUGGESTIONS FOR INTERPRETATION

After line 1 solo 1 jumps up, screams about the room, and disappears. After line 3 solo 2 does the same, and after line 5 solo 3 does the same. Solo 4 appears after line 9. The class is very mysterious and spooky with lines 1, 3, and 5 and very soft but frightened with lines 7, 8, and 9. There is great relief on line 11.

୶ᢒ   SUGGESTIONS FOR ENRICHMENT

Draw scrawny hands or screeching owls.

Discuss and try different kinds of screams.

Talk about nightmares and how frightening but also how unreal they are.

Discuss why darkness sometimes scares adults and children.

A loud scream **SCr**

1. The **screeching** brakes made her **scream**! (all)
2. Aaaaaaaaaaaaaaaah! (solo 1)
3. The **scrawny** hand made her **scramble**! (all)
4. Aaaaaaaaaaaaaaah! (solo 2)
5. The **screeching** owl made him **scrunch**! (all)
6. Aaaaaaaaaaaah! (solo 3)
7. Ooooooooh! A **scream** on the street! (all)
8. Ooooooooh! A **scramble** in the night! (all)
9. Ooooooooh! A **scrunch** in the forest! (all)
10. Dring! Dring! Time to get up boys and girls. (solo 4)
11. Wow! What a dream!!! (all)

❧ REVIEW OF WORDS

screeching	scrawny	scrunch
scream	scramble	

꜇§   SUGGESTIONS FOR STAGING

Solos 1 and 2 stand in front or center of the room.

꜇§   SUGGESTIONS FOR INTERPRETATION

Solo 1 speaks with much anguish and fear. Solo 2 holds his hand. The class stands on line 11 and applauds after line 11.

꜇§   SUGGESTIONS FOR ENRICHMENT

Discuss splinter experiences and the courage it takes to hold still while a needle is digging it out.

Encourage role-playing. Some children can grimace in pain and suffer with a splinter, while others can be reassuring parents or doctors who carefully remove the splinters. If you have a camera handy, take photographs of small groups of faces of children who are pretending they are having splinters removed.

Invite the school nurse to the classroom for a visit. She can explain and demonstrate what needs to be done when a splinter has to be removed.

Ouch!
it hurts!

spl

1. Ouch! It hurts! (solo 1)
2. The **splinter's** in my hand! (solo 1)
3. Stop **spluttering** and hold your hand still. (all)
4. She will get the **splinter** out! (all)
5. Ouch. It hurts! (solo 1)
6. The **splinter's** in my hand! (solo 1)
7. Stop **spluttering** and hold your hand still. (all)
8. She will get the **splinter** out! (all)
9. There! The **splinter** is out! (solo 2)
10. That was **splendid** of you! (solo 1)
11. Yes, very **splendid** of you! (all)

❧ REVIEW OF WORDS

splinter	spluttering	splendid

✍ SUGGESTIONS FOR STAGING

Solo 4, the long leather strap, solo 3, the small piece of string, and solo 2, the tiny bit of straw, are on the floor in the front or middle of the room before the playlet begins. Solo 1 follows the directions of the class. The piece of straw and the piece of string say their lines as they float away in the wind. The leather strap stays put as it says its lines.

✍ SUGGESTIONS FOR INTERPRETATION

Line 11 should be very loud, and on line 12 everyone waves his arms vigorously. On lines 13 and 14 the straw and the string should float about the room. Solo 4 delivers lines 15 and 16 very sadly. Line 17 should fade away as the wind disappears.

✍ SUGGESTIONS FOR ENRICHMENT

Draw pictures of the wind blowing the straw and string into funny or strange places.

Give children small pieces of straw, leather, or string, and let them make a picture incorporating the materials.

Notice things the wind does. Have a child stand in front of a fan and observe what happens when the wind blows. Perhaps a hat could blow off.

List some other good and bad effects of the wind, i.e., it cools, but sometimes it destroys people's houses.

Nevermore!
nevermore!

str

1. As she was walking down the **street** (all)
2. She found a leather **strap**. (all)
3. I found a leather **strap**. (solo 1)
4. And on the **strap** (all)
5. Right on the end (all)
6. She found a piece of **string**. (all)
7. I found a piece of **string**. (solo 1)
8. And on the end of that old **string** (all)
9. She found a piece of **straw**. (all)
10. I found a piece of **straw**. (solo 1)
11. And then there came a great **strong** wind! (all)
12. Whoosh! Whoosh! Whoosh! (all)
13. Away flew the **straw**! (solo 2)
14. Away flew the **string**! (solo 3)
15. "Come back little **straw**," said the leather **strap**. (solo 4)
16. "Come back little **string**," said the leather **strap**. (solo 4)
17. The **strong** wind said, "Nevermore! Nevermore!" (all)

⋘ REVIEW OF WORDS

street	string	strong
strap	straw	

Section Four:
DIGRAPHS

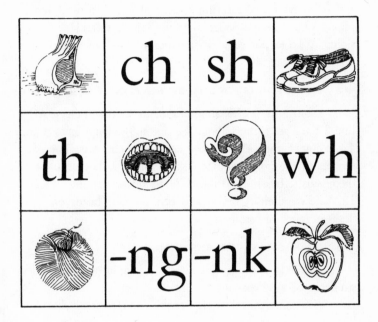

	ch	sh	
	th		wh
	-ng	-nk	

SUGGESTIONS FOR STAGING

Solo 1 should be in the front of the room sitting on a chair or table and creating a carnival atmosphere. A megaphone would be a wonderful prop. Solo 2 should be out of sight. A large pot or a wastepaper basket can contain the imaginary food.

SUGGESTIONS FOR INTERPRETATION

Solo 1 makes his announcements loud and clear. After line 2 the class gathers about the pot and delivers lines 3 and 4. At line 5 they all scamper back to their seats. The class returns to the pot after line 7. After line 9 they go back to their seats. After line 10 the children slowly say lines 11 and 12, holding their tummies and resting their heads on their desks in much discomfort.

SUGGESTIONS FOR ENRICHMENT

Make humorous drawings of people with extended stomachs because they ate too much.

Eat some chocolate chip cookies and/or some chocolate bits brought in by the teacher.

Plan a large carnival painting. Discuss and list things that go on at carnivals or fairs.

Make megaphones out of construction paper and use them to discover their purpose.

Chew,
chomp,
chew and chomp

ch

1. Lamb **chops**, pork **chops**, and **chocolate chips**.
   (solo 1)
2. Step right up and wet your lips. (solo 1)
3. **Chew! Chomp! Chew** and **Chomp!** (all)
4. **Chew! Chomp! Chew** and **Chomp!** (all)
5. **Children!** What are you doing? (solo 2)
6. Lamb **chops**, pork **chops**, and **chocolate chips**.
   (solo 1)
7. Step right up and wet your lips. (solo 1)
8. **Chew! Chomp! Chew** and **Chomp!** (all)
9. **Chew! Chomp! Chew** and **Chomp!** (all)
10. **Children!** What are you doing? (solo 2)
11. **OOOOH!** We ate too **much!** (all)
12. Too **much! Much** too **much!** (all)

REVIEW OF WORDS

chops	chew	children
chocolate	chomp	much
chips		

ᴥᶘ SUGGESTIONS FOR STAGING

The shoes, shirt, and shadow could be imaginary, of course, but it would be more exciting to have a child hide behind something and make a pair of shoes walk and a shirt fly. If possible, use a light that will cast a shadow on a wall.

ᴥᶘ SUGGESTIONS FOR INTERPRETATION

Half the class jump out of their seats on line 1, and the other half jump up on line 2. On line 6 the class huddles in a corner of the room very frightened. Snap the lights off after line 5 and put on the special effects light.

ᴥᶘ SUGGESTIONS FOR ENRICHMENT

Draw all kinds of shadows.

Go outside and observe shadows in the morning, at noon, and before going home. Measure and chart their various lengths. Learn what makes a shadow.

Put on a slide projector and let the children sit in front of it and trace their shadows. Silhouettes make fine presents for parents.

Cut out characters of a favorite story and, using an overhead projector, have the children tell the story while moving the cutouts around.

Present a shadow show on the wall.

Read shadow poems.

Write about your own shadow.

*A shadow
on the wall*

sh

1. Look! Look at the **shoes**! (half the class)
2. The **shoes** are moving! (other half)
3. Look! Look at the **shirt**! (half the class)
4. The **shirt** is waving! (other half)
5. I'm scared! My **shoulders** are **shaking**! (solo 1)
6. **Shh**! There's a **shadow** on the wall! (all)

❧ REVIEW OF WORDS

shoes	shoulders	shh
shirt	shaking	shadow

~~ೈ SUGGESTIONS FOR STAGING

Solos 1, 2, and 3 are in front of the room pretending to be three jack-in-the-boxes. Three boxes large enough for them to get into would be great but unnecessary—the children can just squat and cover their heads until it is time to jump up. On lines 3, 8, and 13 the class stands up and points and then sits after lines 4, 9, and 14. Solo 1 disappears into his box after line 5, solo 2 disappears after line 10, and solo 3 disappears after line 15.

~~ೈ SUGGESTIONS FOR INTERPRETATION

Solo 1 is very silly. Solo 2 is in pain. Solo 3 is very surprised.

~~ೈ SUGGESTIONS FOR ENRICHMENT

Draw huge thumbs.

Tell the story of Tom Thumb or Thumbelina.

Let a child grasp a clean glass. Then hold it up to a strong light and show that fingerprints have been left on the surface. Talk about police identification using fingerprints.

Roll each child's thumb on an ink pad and roll the inked thumb on a piece of white paper to make fingerprints. Hang the thumb prints under pictures or self-portraits of each child.

th

My thumb

1. **The thimble's** on my **thumb**! (solo 1)
2. **The thimble's** on my **thumb**! (solo 1)
3. **There** it is! **There** it is! (all)
4. **The thimble's** on his **thumb**! (all)
5. **Wrong** finger! (solo 1)
6. **The thorn** is in my **thumb**! (solo 2)
7. **The thorn** is in my **thumb**! (solo 2)
8. **There** it is! **There** it is! (all)
9. **The thorn** is in his **thumb**! (all)
10. Ouch! It hurts! (solo 2)
11. My **thumb** is in my mouth! (solo 3)
12. My **thumb** is in my mouth! (solo 3)
13. **There** it is! **There** it is! (all)
14. His **thumb** is in his mouth! (all)
15. My **thumb** is all wet! (solo 3)

ᕫᔕ REVIEW OF WORDS

the	thumb	thorn
thimble	there	mouth

⊷ৈ   SUGGESTIONS FOR STAGING

Solo 1 is at a desk or table at the front of the room holding a cup. Solo 2 hides behind something, out of sight if possible. The teacher pretends to fill the cup with hot chocolate. On lines 1 and 2 the class sits and on lines 5 and 6 stands up. At lines 9 and 10 the class gathers around the child with the cup.

⊷ৈ   SUGGESTIONS FOR INTERPRETATION

The class becomes louder and louder at each sequence. Solo 2 should sound far away.

⊷ৈ   SUGGESTIONS FOR ENRICHMENT

Draw different size cups with various things attempting to get into or out of them.

Play guessing games with the children guessing what, who, and why is in a cup.

Children could bring in a cup they like from home to display or keep on a rack to use when they want a drink of water. They could also put cutout pictures or small objects in their cups.

*Whippity,
whappity,
whup!*

wh

1. **Whippity, whappity, whup** (all)
2. There's something in your cup. (all)
3. **What's** in my cup? (solo 1)
4. Guess **what**! (solo 2)
5. **Whippity, whappity, whup** (all)
6. There's someone in your cup. (all)
7. **Who** is in my cup? (solo 1)
8. Guess **who**! (solo 2)
9. **Whippity, whappity, whup** (all)
10. There's really someone in your cup. (all)
11. **Why** are you in my cup? (solo 1)
12. Guess **why**! (solo 2)
13. We know **what**, and **who**, and **why**! (all)

✑§ REVIEW OF WORDS

whippity	whup	who
whappity	what	why

◄§ SUGGESTIONS FOR STAGING

Solo 1 should walk around all parts of the room while saying his or her lines. On lines 8, 9, 10, and 11 the class should move about the room searching for the "thing." A loud hooray may be shouted on line 16.

◄§ SUGGESTIONS FOR INTERPRETATION

Solo 1 should be very upset and anxious. Solo 2 is very excited with his or her discovery. Of course, the discovery can be anything the child chooses.

◄§ SUGGESTIONS FOR ENRICHMENT

Draw secret pictures of the "thing" each would choose if he or she played the role of solo 2.

As the class advances in phonic recognition, the teacher could suggest that the thing solo 2 must find is an item that begins with a certain sound.

Ask each child to tell about the good hiding places she or he has when playing hide 'n seek at home.

Write phrases describing how the children felt when they lost something of their own or of someone else's.

What thing? -ng -nk

1. **Think**! **Think**! (solo 1)
2. Did you find the **thing**? (solo 1)
3. **Think**! **Think**! (solo 1)
4. Where did you hide the **thing**? (solo 1)
5. What **thing**? What **thing**? (all)
6. You know! You know! (solo 1)
7. **Think** about the **thing**! (solo 1)
8. We've got to find the **thing**! (all)
9. We've got to find the **thing**! (all)
10. **Think** about the **thing**! (all)
11. **Think** about the **thing**! (all)
12. Hurry and find the **thing**! (solo 1)
13. I found it! (solo 2)
14. I found the **thing**. (solo 2)
15. He found the **thing**! (all)
16. Hooray!!! (all)

✑ REVIEW OF WORDS

think   thing